I0752140

I wish I were home again. Oh dear! Oh dear!" – p. 31.

I WILL BE A LADY:

A BOOK FOR GIRLS.

By MRS. TUTHILL.

"She had a kindly word for all,
And was a patient listener too,
Nor deemed it made her more refined
Her household duties to eschew."
OLD BALLAD.

'Enchanted with Polkas, with waltzes delighted,
Devoted to curling, and frizzing, and flouncing,
Good sense she despises, good manners has slighted,
Herself, ne'ertheless, a fine lady pronouncing."

TWENTY-NINTH EDITION.

BOSTON:
CROSBY, NICHOLS, AND COMPANY.
111 WASHINGTON STREET.
1854.

CONTENTS.

CHAPTER I.

A PLEASANT WELCOME.

Beulah Morris. It is not a pretty name, and yet Beulah was a very pretty girl, and a nice girl too, and as well beloved as if her name had been Isabella, Araminta, or Sophonisba.

It was sunset, a beautiful sunset in June. Beulah was gathering roses. She held the two corners of her white apron in one hand, and with a pair of scissors in the other carefully cut red and white roses into it. The front-yard was filled with flowers that Beulah cultivated, and yet it was not a sweet little cottage before which they grew, but a large, square farm-house, — a red house; there were only two white houses in Baxter, — the minister's and the doctor's.

The town of Baxter was named after that man of blessed memory, whose " last words" were so precious, that after his death, they continued to publish "More Last Words of Richard Baxter." It is a primitive New England village, where the good people have yet only "heard tell" of a rail-road; — where no factories have yet disturbed the pure streams, that, after flowing through the green meadows, dash over the rocks in beautiful cascades. The wells still go with a long sweep, — a pole with "the moss-covered bucket" at one end, and a large stone at the other. The old brown houses are two stories in front, and behind slope almost down to the ground; but Squire Morris's house was a red one, and the rose-bushes had been sent from a distance, many years before, by the Squire's cousin.

Beulah, while filling her white apron, repeated those sweet lines written by Mary Howitt; —

"God might have made the earth bring forth
Enough for great and small,
The oak-tree and the cedar-tree,
And not a flower at all."

Mrs. Morris came to the door. "Beulah, my child," said she, "why do you cut so many flowers? you know I want them for rose-water."

"You spared them this morning, mother, and told me I might have my apron-full; see, it is only just full," replied Beulah, showing her heaped-up treasures; "and you know, as the bushes were sent us by Mrs. Whately, it is no more than right that she should enjoy as many of the roses as she can. See, mother, how beautiful they are. I cannot think they were only made for rose-water, for we might have had that,

'And not a flower at all.'"

"You are a queer child, Beulah, a very queer child. And what are you going to do with the roses?"

"Ornament the white room, the nice spare chamber, for Mrs. Whately," replied the little girl.

"And be laughed at, as a silly little country-girl, for your pains," said the mother.

Beulah could not think so. "The lady would not have sent them so far for a present," said she, "if she did not love roses."

"She knew they were good for rose-water; — but follow your own notion," said Mrs. Morris.

While Beulah flew to the spare chamber to arrange the roses, Mrs. Morris spread her supper-table; — cold ham stood in friendly nearness to sweetmeats, and pickles kept their sourness to themselves by the side of cakes and pies; — the broiled chickens, toast, and hot potatoes waited for the arrival of the visiter.

Squire Morris now came in from the labors of the farm, followed by two stout lads, his sons.

"Well, wife, all in order? — that 's right, — dressed in your Sunday best; I don't think I shall make much change myself, — only try to be a little neater. There 's no comfort in being untidy. Azariah and Medad, if you are ashamed of your every-day clothes, you can rig up a little."

Azariah did not choose to take the trouble, but Medad went to put on his Sunday suit.

While the Squire was performing his ablutions, a plain but handsome carriage, with a pair of sleek black horses, drove up to the door, and all the way down the front-yard to the gate went the Squire, vigorously wiping hands and face.

From the carriage stepped a lady of about thirty-five.

"Well now, cousin Whately, this is kind, to come so far to see us," said the Squire, giving the lady a hearty kiss. Then, seeing there was a very gaily dressed person in the coach, he said, "Is n't the other lady going to get out?"

Mrs. Whately said, in a low tone, "That is one of my domestics;" then, addressing the coachman,

"Thomas, you may drive back to the inn we have just past, with your wife, and remain till I send for you, after you have placed my luggage within the yard."

The man did as he was ordered, while the Squire whispered, "Why do you send them to the tavern; we have room enough for all your folks. Though 't would n't be quite so pleasant for such smart pieces to be in the kitchen with old Cato and his wife."

"I prefer that they should stay there," replied she, and the coachman mounted the box and drove off.

"I 've no doubt they 'll take that smart body for the lady at the tavern," said the Squire, "and she 'll play off her airs at a great rate."

Mrs. Morris received Mrs. Whately with the same cordiality as the Squire had done.

"This is little Beulah," said Mrs. Whately.

"I had no idea that she could be so tall; you must be nearly twelve years old, dear."

"I am quite twelve," replied Beulah.

"I do n't believe you would have known the boys, Azariah and Medad; they will soon be as tall as their father."

"I should not, indeed," replied Mrs. Whately,

looking up to the boys, either of whom would have measured six feet in his stockings, although the oldest was not yet nineteen.

Mrs. Whately was shown into the spare chamber, to take off her travelling-dress, and soon descended to the sitting-room.

The Squire handed round a brimming glass of brandy toddy, which Mrs. Whately declined, saying she did not know that so ancient a custom was yet retained in any part of New England.

"I go for comfort, cousin Whately, and so does my old woman," said the Squire, taking a drink and passing it to the boys. "But come, sit down and try how you can make out a supper from country fare."

Mrs. Whately looked around upon the bountiful table as she sat down, and said, "Your luxurious fare speaks of more than comfort, and some one, Mrs. Morris I suppose, has a love of the beautiful."

Mrs. Morris did not understand the allusion, and blushed without making any reply.

"The roses so tastefully arranged in the room you have appropriated to me look beautifully. The snow-white curtains looped up with the pink roses, and the white ones laid along the dark mantel, have a charming effect. Their perfume, too, gave me a delicious welcome."

"O, that was some of Beulah's nonsense," said the mother.

"How came you to think of that, child?" inquired the father.

"The flowers that I love so dearly," replied Beulah, "I have often been told were sent to us by Mrs. Whately, and I thought it would please her to find they were still as beautiful as ever."

"Why, she spends half her time when out of school in tending them," said Mrs. Morris, laughing, "and she often talks to them as if they were living beings."

"I am glad they have given you so much pleasure," said Mrs. Whately. The sweet smile that accompanied the words Beulah did not perfectly understand, but it went bright and warm to her heart, like a sunbeam into one of her own roses.

CHAPTER II.

THE PUZZLING WORD.

Long before daylight the next morning, Mrs. Whately was awakened by a variety of sounds, very different from those to which she was accustomed. She could sleep in spite of the rattling of carts over the paved street, but the farm-yard chorus of cows, pigs, turkeys, chickens, geese, and guinea-hens was quite too much for her. She arose and enjoyed that beautiful sight, so seldom seen in the city, — a glorious sunrise. The first civility offered her on descending to the "sitting-room" was a glass of bitters.

"No, no; Cousin Joab, do not offer me any thing of the kind; I never drank ardent spirits in my life, and it would not be well to begin just as every one else is leaving off. Have n't you a Temperance Society yet in Baxter?"

"No, we have n't; our minister says, we hard-working folks require a little spirits now and then," replied the Squire.

"That accounts for your having formed no society of that kind. He probably indulges himself in the use of it."

"He takes a *leetle*, a very *leetle*, occasionally," was the reply.

"I am sorry to hear it, because his example is important to his parishioners," said Mrs. Whately.

"There is our Beulah, now," said the mother; "she has read some of those temperance stories, and she would n't drink a drop for the world."

Again that smile of approbation from Mrs. Whately made the little girl's heart throb with pleasure.

While they were at breakfast, in rushed a young girl without any ceremony, and, throwing her bonnet aside, took a vacant seat at the table.

"Do n't you see the lady, Finey," said Squire Morris.

The girl scarcely looked up, but, bowing slightly, said, "How d' ye do, Ma'am," and commenced eating with a right good appetite the nice things that the Squire heaped upon her plate.

She was dressed in an old, faded satin, a rich

material so disfigured that it was almost impossible to tell that the original color was purple. The bonnet, too, of yellow silk, was made for an older person, and had been *razeed* to suit the present wearer; in consequence of frequent exposure to all sorts of weather, the artificial flowers had streaked it red and green.

" What a forlorn specimen of the shabby genteel," thought Mrs. Whately.

" Take another piece of beefsteak, Finey," said the Squire; " I like to see you take comfort."

" And Finey will take a drink of cider ? " said Medad, laying his hand upon a large pitcher.

" No, I thank you, Mr. Medad; I prefer coffee," replied the girl; " but I wish you would not call me Finey; I do n't admire any thing fine; and besides, I do n't like that *young* men should speak to me in that manner."

" Good," said Azariah, striking the table with his fist till the crockery fairly danced; " call him Daddy."

" I shall do no such thing," replied she, blushing; " I would not be so impertinent. Do not think, because I am such a wild harum-scarum, that I have no sense of propriety."

Mrs. Whately was much amused by this con

versation. "Your young friend," said she to Beulah, "seems to have some very just notions. You must introduce us to each other."

Beulah did not understand the ceremony of an introduction, but her young visiter did, and, looking for the first time into Mrs. Whately's face, she was much surprised to see an exceedingly lady-like stranger. She blushed deeply as she said, "My name, Madam, is Zephina Fanshaw. I was named for my father;—his name was Zephaniah. I hope you will excuse my rudeness, and you, too, Mrs. Morris, in not noticing there was a stranger at table." Then, rising hastily, she continued, "Will you allow Beulah to walk a little distance with me, Mrs. Morris,—just down the field behind the house."

"Yes, Zephina, but you must not keep her long," was the reply.

"Certainly not, when she has so much reason to wish to be at home," said Zephina, looking at Mrs. Whately.

"Beulah is going to show me her flowers while the dew is upon them, this morning," said Mrs. Whately.

"Come, Beulah dear, make haste, then; I 'll not letain you long," said she, and the faded yellow

2

bonnet was tossed on the head, receiving a glance of ineffable scorn from its wearer, who, bidding a hasty "good morning," left the house, followed by Beulah.

They had gone but a few steps from the house when Zephina said, "Pray tell me, Beulah, who that woman is at your house?"

"It is my father's cousin, Mrs. Whately."

"Your father's cousin!" exclaimed Zephina; "they do n't look any more alike than an oyster and a cream-cake. I wonder that I did not notice her when I came in. Your father is so kind and helps me to so many good things that I can see nothing else. But I shall enjoy no more of these nice times, for mamma has forbidden me to go any more to your house, because she says country folks are all vulgar. Now do n't be angry, Beulah, because she does not know your family, a single one of them; if she did she could n't help loving you all as I do; and you know it is my only pleasure to see you, and come to your house."

"I am very sorry, Zephina, but I am not angry, for I do not know what your mother means by vulgar," said Beulah.

"Only not genteel," replied Zephina, while

the large tears rolled out upon her cheeks; "poor mamma wishes to make me a lady, but she never will succeed, never. I may sit with my toes turned out and my shoulders braced back to a board, practise on the piano four hours a day and study four more, and yet not become a lady. I like much better to enjoy the country and the good honest country folks. They are as happy again as the city folks that I used to see; I remember their cross, proud looks."

"But Mrs. Whately is from the city," said Beulah, "and she does not look cross and proud."

"That she does not. She is a lovely woman. I would not call her a lady for any thing, for I hate the very name. But, Beulah, she is waiting for you, and we must part. I shall come often to this old oak-tree. This shall be our place of meeting, and our post-office, too; for I mean to write to you, and you must answer my letters."

"I will try," said Beulah; and they threw their arms around each other's necks. A dozen kisses were interchanged, and they parted.

"I do n't know much about them," said the Squire in answer to Mrs. Whately's inquiry, "Who are the Fanshaws?" "Nobody seems to make out much, though it is n't for want of prying. Mrs. Fanshaw is a widow, and Finey is her only child. They live down at the cottage, as they call it, about half a mile off. I like Finey, and I love dearly to see her eat, for I 've got a notion that she is kept on short allowance at home. I 've asked her to come and take a meal with us often, and she generally drops in about this time in the morning, before her mother is up, I reckon."

"She is always dressed in some such old Crazy-Kate finery as she had on this morning," said Mrs. Morris; "I never saw her have on any thing fit for a respectable young girl in my life."

"And yet, for all that, she looks better than any girl in our meeting-house," said Medad.

Beulah returned home sad and thoughtful. Her mild hazel eyes, usually so clear, were red with weeping.

"Why, what ails my darling?" said the Squire.

Beulah replied at once, "Mrs. Fanshaw has forbidden Zephina to come here any more."

"That, indeed!" said he. "Well, we can do much better without her than she can without us. She will look leaner and paler than ever now. Did she give any reason for this?"

"She did, but I had rather not mention it," said Beulah, almost weeping. That word "vulgar" applied to her dear parents; how could any one be so cruel! Yet she did not understand it.

"This is very strange, child," said Mrs Morris. "You must not look so sorrowful. Mrs. Whately has been waiting for you a long time, to show her your beloved flowers."

"Come, Beulah," said Mrs. Whately, "the sun will soon rob your favorites of their freshness;" and, taking Beulah by the hand, they went out together.

"I am going to ask you a question, Mrs. Whately," said Beulah, after they had been some time in the garden. "And yet I do not know that it would be quite right.'

"Ask any question that you please of me," kindly replied Mrs. Whately.

Thus encouraged, Beulah commenced, "Zephina's mother will not allow her to come to our house because she thinks we are vulgar; will you please to tell me what that ugly word means?"

Mrs. Whately hesitated a moment, and her young companion whispered, "Is it because our family drink spirits? I saw you did not approve of that, and I have thought for some time that it was not right."

"That practice is, in these days, considered vulgar by many, and I hope your family will soon give it up," was the reply.

"I will try to persuade them to do it," quickly replied the amiable girl.

Mrs. Whately did not think it right to let the matter pass thus, and added, "There are many ways in which the word is used, but incorrectly; nothing is really vulgar excepting what is mean, improper, or wicked. Some mistaken persons apply it to those who do not live in an elegant and stylish manner. Zephina's mother probably used it in this sense. You have felt, my dear Beulah, that there is a glory and a beauty in the works of creation, — that many things are not alone useful, — that this world, with its glorious sky, and its green hills and valleys, its woods and its beautiful flowers, was not made thus, merely for a place to eat, drink, work, and sleep in, but that the beings for whom it was made so excellent might admire and enjoy it, and lift up grateful hearts to the beneficent Creator; and, as in the natural world there is this beauty, so in human character, in the heart itself, there may be such goodness and such refinement as to give a bloom and beauty to the actions."

Although Beulah Morris did not perfectly understand Mrs. Whately, yet there was something in her very soul that responded to the sentiments of her new friend. She was silent and thoughtful for a while, then her large, soft eyes looked earnestly in Mrs. Whately's face as she said; "The kindness of my father and mother is beautiful to me."

CHAPTER III

ZEPHINA'S MAMMA.

At a rattling old piano sat the disconsolate Zephina, laboring over a piece of music. Her mother's patience, never very remarkable, was now quite exhausted.

"You are the most stupid girl in the world, Zephina," she exclaimed; "you will never be fit for fashionable society."

"From all I know of fashionable society, stupidity would fit me better for it than any thing else," pettishly replied Zephina.

"This all comes from your being so much of late with those Homespuns in that horrid red house. Did you tell them I could not permit you to come there again?" inquired her mother.

"I did," replied Zephina. "I had a nice breakfast first, and then how mean, how cruel, it was to tell Beulah that I could not come to see her again because country folks are vulgar. She is much more genteel now than I am, or ever shall be. She looks sweetly in her snow-white aprons and homespun frocks. I prophesy that she will one day make as elegant a woman as her father's cousin, Mrs. Whately."

"And who is she?"

"A very lovely woman whom I saw there this morning, dressed so neatly, — so — I do n't know what to call it, for I hate the word *genteelly*. And then her carriage, that dark green coach, with the rich hammer-cloth, and the coal-black horses, — all plain, yet so very elegant."

"And you say this was the Homespuns' cousin?" eagerly inquired Mrs. Fanshaw.

"Squire Morris's cousin, I said, mamma, and she had none of the fixed-up look that I do so abominate. Please give me something to wear besides this old trumpery, — these old silk dresses and Madge Wildfire bonnets."

"I wish I had known before that there was such a lady visiting at the farm-house," said Mrs. Fanshaw, without taking any notice of her daughter's request. "Cannot you make some excuse to call again and find out something more about her?"

"No, mamma; I cannot degrade myself by such meanness; — they are kind-hearted excellent people; — the nice old Squire; I love him dearly. I did not say the fine woman that I saw there was a lady; — you know I never call people that I like ladies."

"O Zephina, you have such shockingly low tastes," in a piteous tone whined Mrs. Fanshaw. "I do not know what will become of you; I think I shall call on the lady myself."

"You, mamma! why should you?"

"Why, if her equipage is so splendid as you say it is, she must be somebody." was the reply.

"If it is the carriage and horses that you respect so much, you can call upon them at the tavern, for there is where I saw them," said Zephina.

"You are a very provoking girl, Zephina, and I can never make you understand these things."

"O mamma, excuse my impertinence; I know it is wrong, but indeed I do see too plainly into the ways of the world; — I am old before my time."

Mrs. Fanshaw made no reply, but went to array herself to call on the stranger.

The style of Mrs. Fanshaw's dress somewhat resembled that of Zephina, though the materials were not of such undeniable antiquity. The satin shoes, with which she saw fit to make her way among the stones, had to suffer; and her long veil, floating far behind her, caught repeatedly upon the briers by the road-side. From her sallow complexion, and the expression of discontent and affectation upon her countenance, one would have judged that the pure sources of health and happiness were lost to her; — that face it was painful to behold.

When she arrived at the farm-house, she had entirely forgotten the lady's name, and was obliged to inquire for Mrs. Morris. Beulah, who came to the door, said that her mother was not at home; she had gone to see a sick neighbour.

"Is the lady at home who is visiting here? Mrs. — what is her name?"

"Mrs. Whately?" said Beulah; "she is here. Will you walk in?"

Mrs. Fanshaw did so; and, handing her card to Beulah, said; "That is a card, with my name on it, girl; give it to the lady." Then, as she took a seat in the little parlour, and glanced at the home-made carpet and plain furniture, the marked smile of contempt that distorted her mouth called up a rosy blush to the face of Beulah Morris.

As soon as Mrs. Whately had read the name,—"Mrs. Zephaniah Fanshaw,"—she quietly laid the card upon the table, saying, "Beulah, dear, please say to the lady, that, as I stay so short a time in Baxter, I receive no ceremonious visits."

Beulah gave the message very politely, and Mrs. Fanshaw stalked out of the house with an air of offended pride, much more ridiculous than sublime.

"How did you like Mrs. Whately?" inquired Zephina.

"She was engaged, I presume; but the farmer's girl, not understanding etiquette, gave me a very singular excuse. It was not genteel in the person — not genteel at all — to send an apology; and I dare say the carriage is only a hired hack, after all."

This singular mode of reasoning amused Zephina exceedingly; but she made no reply. She went to her room and wrote a letter, which, early the next morning, was conveyed to the post-office, under the old oak-tree.

CHAPTER IV.

GIRLISH CORRESPONDENCE

ZEPHINA'S LETTER.

"DEAR, sweet little Beulah, — rose-bud of all rose-buds for me. — Was n't it the funniest thing for mamma to call at your house? I laughed and laughed till the tears ran out of my eyes, to think how you would stare to see her coming up the yard. What a funny, funny world this is! I, poor I, am nothing but every-day stuff, just fit for every-day wear; and yet am to be made a lady, *bon gré, mal gré*, that is, whether I will or no; and you, dearest Beulah, who are of such nice, delicate stuff, that you are fit for Sundays and holydays, may live always in the country, and care not a fig what any body thinks of you, excepting those you love.

"Tell me all about that good woman, Mrs.

Whately. She has such a sweet voice, and such simple, natural manners, that I want to see her again very much. You know I have always lived in a large city till a short time since, and, of course, have seen a great many people. If there were more of them like Mrs. Whately, it would not be such a comical world as it is.

"Give my compliments to the green carriage and the black horses; they ought, after, or before, the owner, to command my respect. But somehow I do find it difficult to think any more of a person merely because they ride in a carriage, than if they went on foot.

"Tell the Squire that I did not love him for the nice things he gave me, but because he is such a dear, kind soul. Yet I confess to a love of 'the goodies' too. Now write as you promised, and put it in the post-office for your own

"ZEPHINA.

"P. S. Tell me, Beulah, did Mrs. Whately laugh at my forlorn old bonnet, with those old flowers, gone to seed ages ago?"

The next morning Zephina flew to the old oak, and there upon the stone was a basket of cakes, and under the basket the following note.

"DEAR ZEPHINA: —

"Mrs. Whately did not laugh at your bonnet. I do not believe she would make fun of any body, let them wear what they would. I should like to tell you a great many sweet, pretty things that she says of you, but I have not time, for that good woman, as you call her, goes home to-morrow, and I want to see her as much as I can. I must tell you, though, she says we must still be good friends, and that I must let her know all about our post-office, and every thing we do, after she is at home again. Only think, Zephina, I have got to write to her, and you see what a poor hand I am at letter-writing. In a great hurry. From yours, always, BEULAH.

"P. S. Leave the little basket with your next letter, that I may fill it again."

Beulah had fortunately had a good master at the district-school that she attended every winter; she wrote a pretty, neat hand, and her partial friend was even more delighted with the note than with the seedcakes.

Mrs. Whately's visit had given great pleasure to all the Morris family. Medad said, she had such a kind way of persuading him into it, that he could not help giving up spirits and cider. The Squire thought he should come round in time, and even Azariah said there was no holding out against such a woman's good advice.

Beulah felt very lonely after her departure, and daily went to the old oak-tree for a letter from her young friend. To her great joy, on the third morning the empty basket was there and a full letter.

ZEPHINA'S SECOND LETTER.

"DEAREST AND SWEETEST: —

"There is no end of funny things. Mamma has now got her hands full. An old acquaintance of hers — a man who has some way or other made considerable property in the country, and has lately moved to New York — has sent his daughter to be taught good manners. Actually sent her for *two months* to be taught '*good breeding*, good manners, and all that sort of thing,' as he expresses it.

"Now I always thought that good breeding meant the way in which a person was brought up, all the way along; but I do n't know but Harriet Ann Gunn (for that 's her name) can take it suddenly, just as one does the measles or whooping-cough. I wish you could see this Harriet Ann make a courtesy. Out slides the right foot about a yard, then up jerks the other behind it, then down, down, slowly goes the little lady till you do n't know where she will stop; then she comes up with a sudden flying out of both hands to help her rise. O, dear! It is enough to kill a body to see this performance. But I have n't told you how she looks: — Hair, white and straight as candles; eyes, blue as glass beads, staring right at you; neck, long and thin; nose, just enough of it to be called a nose; mouth, good enough for every purpose; ears, large and white.

"There, now, you have Harriet Ann. She looks in the glass forty times a day to practise that amazing courtesy, and tumbles over on her face almost as often, trying to stand with her toes turned straight out. She has just left off pantalettes, and feels very consequential in long dresses; but does not know yet how to manage them. However, she thinks long dresses make her at once a young lady. O Beulah! but you ought to hear her say 'beaucheful,' and 'I keant,' and 'garding,' and 'kitching,' and ever so many such words. You must see her; I declare you must. To-morrow morning I will walk by just after breakfast with her, and if Mr. Medad could only be at home, it would be capital fun to see that courtesy that can't be described.

"I could n't write before because of the coming of this Harriet Ann. Do n't trouble yourself to fill the basket. I am afraid you think I am a greedy little thing for a girl of thirteen.

"Remember, to-morrow morning by seven o'clock be on the look out. Your loving

"ZEPHINA."

CHAPTER V.

AIRS AND GRACES.

"SURE enough, there they come!" said Medad the next morning, as Beulah and himself were at the window.

The tall, thin girl, with China-blue eyes, was dressed in a bright pink merino, and her winter bonnet, with red feathers, though it was June, — because the country folks would not know but that was the city fashion.

As soon as Zephina saw Medad and Beulah, she said, "There are some acquaintances of mine; make your courtesy, Harriet Ann."

And accordingly out went the foot for a long slide, and all the rest just as Zephina described it and down went the long, pink merino into the dust, leaving a dark border around it. Beulah could not refrain from smiling, and Medad's

"Haw, haw, haw," might have been heard half a mile. But Miss Harriet Ann, quite delighted with herself, had not a suspicion of the cause, and stretching her long neck to its greatest extent, strutted off like a young turkey.

"What a pretty garding!" she exclaimed. "Was that a young gent'man at the window? I was n't quite certing, but I thought I saw one?"

"Poor girl! it 's too bad to laugh at her," said Beulah; "she did her very best."

"No doubt of that; and 't was worth a dollar to see this," replied Medad, giving a faithful imitation of the courtesy as he left the room.

Zephina and her companion had not gone far, before they met a number of cows going leisurely to pasture.

"See those horrid crichures!" exclaimed Harriet Ann; "I 'm scared to death. What shall I do?"

"Jump over the fence," said Zephina.

"I can't, to save my life," said the girl, wringing her hands, screaming, and running back.

The boy who was driving the cows had the mischievous spirit too often found in boys, and commenced driving them faster. Harriet Ann ran through mud and mire as fast as she could. First she lost one shoe, then the other; at length, a dog came towards her, barking, — the cows in full chase behind, the dog in front. What could she do? She tried to climb the fence, but her dress caught, when she had got one foot over, and there she sat, screaming and screeching, "This nasty country! I wish I was home again. O, dear! O, dear!"

Her bonnet now blew off; the dog snatched it up and shook it at a fearful rate. Forgetful of her alarm, she scrambled down and seized hold of it; but the dog kept his teeth tightly shut upon it, and Harriet Ann and he were having a fierce contest, each pulling with all their might, when Medad, whose dog it was, came up, and calling "Rover, Rover, at them!" the dog went after the cows, and they were soon out of sight.

The velvet bonnet was torn and bent into the most comical form, its bright red feathers broken, and draggled in the mire. She however stuck it upon the top of her head, for it was too much bent for the head to gain admittance; and then she went off into that courtesy, saying, "You 've saved my life," — bonnet, she ought to have said, — "and I am unaffectedly obliged to you."

Z phina had now come up with them; she leaned against the fence, fcr she laughed so im moderately that she could not stand up, while Medad coughed violently, holding his handkerchief to his mouth. But the cough would end in a "Haw, haw," in spite of him.

"Suppose we go and fish for the lost shoes," seid Zephina, as soon as she could stop laughing; pointing at the stocking-feet, all covered with mud.

"I 'll help you," said Medad.

After poking around for some time, the shoes were found full of mud; but it was impossible for Harriet Ann to put them on. The stones hurt her feet, so that at length she began to cry; "O, dear! O, dear! I never can walk so far."

"Poor girl!" exclaimed Zephina, who began really to pity her; "we 'll make a lady-chair and carry you. Come, Mr. Medad, you know how."

So they placed their hands together and made the lady-chair, and Harriet Ann was carried safely to Mrs. Fanshaw's door.

No sooner had Medad left, than she said, "That 's a very polite gent'man. Does he go in the fust society in Baxter?"

"Certingly," said Zephina.

The exclamations of Mrs. Fanshaw, on seeing the shocking plight in which Miss Harriet Ann returned, frightened her more than either cows or dog had done. "How disgusting! how unlady-like! how awkward! how careless!" A perfect volley was poured forth upon the tattered and mud-bespattered damsel.

"I thought it was lady-like to be timid," said Zephina, partly out of good nature, hoping to divert the torrent of rebuke from Harriet Ann. "Those terrific *crichures*, the cows, how could they fail to frighten a girl half out of her wits, who has lived in the city two whole years?"

"It is better to have a little delicate timidity, than to be utterly fearless, as you are, Zephina," replied her mother. "Harriet Ann has a nervous sensibility that may render her quite interesting as a young lady."

Thus encouraged, Harriet Ann had a thousand little "Ahs," and "Ohs," and "Dear mes," and shrill shrieks, at the sight of such harmless things as bees and butterflies, and a caterpillar or a toad would throw her almost into convulsions. These ridiculous fears were a perpetual annoyance to

Zephina, who was fond of looking at innocent and often beautiful insects, which Harriet Ann, with "delicate timidity," called "nasty and disgusting things."

CHAPTER VI.

FRIENDLY SUGGESTIONS.

Soon after Mrs. Whately returned home she wrote Beulah the following letter.

"My Dear Beulah: —

"I have thought very often of you since we parted. I had a pleasant journey home. Yet I think that my home seems more solitary than ever since my return.

"I remember you asked me the day before I left you, if I disliked the name *lady;* saying that your young friend disliked it very much. I did not answer you then; I will do so now.

"I do not dislike it, Beulah, yet I should not wish to be called a *fine lady;* a *fine woman* would be a much more complimentary term. Yet every one would desire to be called *lady-like;* tha would be understood to mean something refined and dignified. It is a high compliment, too, to say of a woman that she is a perfect lady, though the term has been often misused. A perfect lady has delicacy of sentiment and delicacy of taste. She would do nothing mean, nor disgusting, nor undignified; nothing, in short, that would produce self-contempt. She wishes not only to appear to others delicate and refined, but to be so, for her own sake. She would pay great attention to the feelings of others, that she might not wound them in any way. This, and much more, springs from delicacy of sentiment. In her dress, manners, and every thing belonging to her condition as a woman, she would manifest a certain propriety, that we call delicacy of taste.

"We should perform our duty to God, my dear Beulah, not that we may be called good or pious, but simply because it is our duty, and because we love Him who has a right to our obedience.

"In the same manner, we should perform our whole duty to ourselves, because it exalts us as rational beings, and makes us more happy. We should be kind and polite to others, not to gain the name of a lady, but because we love our fellow-beings, and wish to do them good.

"All these things I hope you will understand in time. Confide to me any difficulties you may encounter, and I will try to solve them. There is nothing so lovely in a woman as an amiable disposition. A very distinguished author said, 'Of all external objects a graceful person is the most agreeable; in vain will a person attempt to be graceful who is deficient in amiable qualities.' I am afraid your young friend Zephina, from her dislike of fine ladies, has fallen into an opposite extreme, and is in danger of being rude and hoydenish. This her good sense will, I trust, in time, correct; for Pope says, 'Good manners are the blossoms of good sense.'

"I send you, dear Beulah, a dressing-case. It is for every-day use. Combs, hair-brush, tooth-brush, and nail-brush; — may they do you excellent service. Exquisite neatness will make even a plain girl look charmingly in my eyes.

"There are some trifles, too, marked with the names of the friends for whom they are designed, which I beg you, dear, to present in the name of your sincere friend, LAURA WHATELY."

"Why can't I be a lady?" thought Beulah Morris

CHAPTER VII.

FREE AND EASY.

Beulah was gathering strawberries, — "red, ripe strawberries." Zephina and Harriet Ann were taking a morning walk. Beulah was stooping down, and so busily occupied that she did not observe the girls approach.

Harriet Ann stepped up to her and said, "Little girl, give me some of your strawberries, will you?"

Beulah handed her the basket, which was half full, and she commenced eating them voraciously.

Zephina stood off at a little distance to enjoy the interview. Beulah seated herself upon a large stone, while Harriet Ann continued to devour the berries.

"What horribly thick shoes you wear, girl!

Have n't you got any better ones?" inquired Harriet Ann.

"They answer my purpose very well," replied Beulah.

"Certingly, they are just right for one who has to go about picking berries among all these nasty stones and briers, but how queer they would look in Broadway. And what a strange dress you have on; I mean how queer it is made. You do n't have the costumes here very often I suppose. Who is your dress-maker?"

"My mother," replied Beulah.

"Is she a dress-maker by trade? I never heard there was such a thing in this vulgar place. Does she go out by the day, or take in work?"

"She has no reason for going out, since she makes only her own dresses and mine," replied Beulah.

"That is so queer, now; I suppose she is too poor to hire a dress-maker. Was you ever in any place but this horrid Baxter?"

"This place is very pleasant to me, since I have seen no other excepting the neighbouring town of Perkinsville," answered Beulah, with perfect coolness.

The strawberries were nearly all eaten.

"Where can Zephina be all this time," said Harriet Ann, handing back the basket, and about to offer Beulah one cent!

At the name of her friend she sprang up, and, Zephina jumping out from behind a large sweet-brier bush, they were soon in each other's arms.

"Come," said Zephina, after almost smothering Beulah with kisses, "come, dearest, let us go to work and fill your basket again. I 'll help you make up what that city lady has devoured. Was n't it fun alive to hear that dialogue?" and she began picking with all her might.

"Do n't trouble yourself, Zephina, for it is your own loss. I happened to see some uncommonly fine strawberries just here this morning, and thought I would gather some for you."

"So, then, Miss Harriet Ann Gunn, I do n't thank you at all for cramming down my fruit. I wish you could see yourself, with your face stained from ear to ear."

The girl's eyes opened wider than ever with astonishment to think this was Zephina's friend Beulah, of whom she had heard her talk so much; but she stood speechless, trying to recollect what she had said while eating the berries.

"Well, Beulah, do n't mind about the loss to

me; we must go home now. Good by, little girl; does your mother go out, or take in work at home?" imitating exactly Harriet Ann's voice and manner.

> "Is this the world of which I want a sight?
> Are these the beings who are called polite?"

Beulah might have said as she wended her way homeward, for such were her thoughts.

She was no sooner out of hearing than Harriet Ann began,—"You do n't say, Zephina, that such an unbecomingly dressed crichure as that belongs to the fust society. It can't be. I thought she was some poor body picking berries for a living."

"And so you thought you would help her, by eating them all up?" said Zephina.

"Why, I was just going to offer her a cent, as she jumped up at the sound of your name."

"Merciful me!" exclaimed Zephina; "one cent, for what was worth a shilling, if she had been picking them for her living. One cent! I wonder what the generous Squire would have said to that. It 's too good a joke, and yet I 'm glad Beulah did not see it."

"If folks are any thing or any body, I say they

ought to dress so that other folks who are somebody may know it," said Harriet Ann.

"A very neatly worded sentence! About as clear as your notions of gentility."

"Do n't be angry, Zephina; I am sorry I ate up your strawberries," said Harriet Ann.

"Do you think I care for the loss of a few strawberries?" replied Zephina, almost fiercely. "No, not a bit. It is because you insulted my dearest friend. I endured your impertinence as long as I could; but if I had seen the grand flourish at the end of it, I verily believe I should have forgotten myself, and boxed your ears soundly."

"I hope I shall never see the girl again," whimpered out Harriet Ann.

"I hope in all conscience you never will," was the reply.

But this was not the only annoyance inflicted by Harriet Ann during the two months of her visitation. Zephina could not write to Beulah, without being surprised at seeing a long braid of light hair hanging over her own shoulder, and, upon looking up, there were those great blue eyes staring right down upon the paper. When told that it was very bad manners to look over a person who was writing, Harriet Ann would say; "I think I have a right to look over you, for I know you are going to say something about me." If Zephina, when very much interested in a book, chanced to lay it down for a moment, up it was snatched by the impertinent visiter, and detained to rest her elbow upon it, as long as she saw fit, in spite of the longing looks of the impatient reader.

Mrs. Fanshaw kept but one *domestic*, and as that was the name universally given to those who went out to service in Baxter, Lucy, a good, honest Yankee girl, chose to be called a domestic; but Harriet Ann, in opposition to the request of Mrs. Fanshaw, always called her a *servant*. 'Will you order your servant to do this or that?" was repeated twenty times a day in Lucy's presence. At one time she would treat this girl with the greatest contempt, and give out her orders in the most imperious manner; then she would be on terms of the greatest familiarity and even intimacy, borrowing from her articles of wearing apparel, such as collars and pocket-handkerchiefs.

Lucy, too, was made the confidant of all her grievances. She never saw such a mean woman as Mrs. Fanshaw; they did n't have any thing good to eat; they must be dreadfully poor; she wondered how Lucy could ever expect to have her wages paid; they were not genteel people at all.

At the dinner-table she would look at every dish with a dissatisfied, contemptuous expression, which made her upper lip almost touch her nose; and, when offered any thing, would perhaps consent to take a little *meat* and a little rice, saying, however, she never ate such things at home.

> " She takes what she at first professed to loath,
> And in due time feeds heartily on both;
> Yet, still o'erclouded with a constant frown,
> She does not swallow, but she gulps it down."

She called all animal food *meat*, or *fowls*, or *fish;* and when Mrs. Fanshaw told her she should always name the kind of meat, — as beef, mutton, &c., — or of birds, — as turkey, duck, chicken — or of fish, — as salmon, haddock, &c., — Harriet Ann was quite offended, and said she did not know one from the other; and if she did, she should be mistaken in New York for a butcher's daughter. She knew they never did so in the city, or if they used to when Mrs. Fanshaw lived there, they did n't now. This was her unfailing, and, in her opinion, unanswerable argument "They do n't do so in the city," or "They do so in the city."

She never troubled herself to wipe her feet on the mat at the door, and would come in with them covered with mud, and, drawing one of them under, would settle herself upon Mrs. Fanshaw's ottoman without the least hesitation. This, her habitual mode of sitting, with one foot under her, was vastly inconvenient; for, when obliged to rise in haste, she was in danger of pitching head first upon the floor, and finding herself with a flattened nose.

Heartily glad were Mrs. Fanshaw and her daughter when the day of Harriet Ann's departure arrived. The two months had expired. A short time indeed to teach good manners to one habitually ill-bred, and so conceited withal, as to suppose herself the very personification of *gentility!* Years of teaching, both by precept and example, would have had but little effect upon Harriet Ann Gunn.

She dressed herself for the journey in that selfsame soiled pink merino in which she had first appeared, with all her gaudy trinkets about her person, — ear-rings, bracelets, and all. When the stagecoach drove up to the door, she handed Lucy an old faded hair-ribbon, that she had done wearing herself, for a present. And when Lucy looked at it with surprise, she said, " Why do n't you make a courtesy, girl, and say ' Thank you, Ma'am ' ? Ha' n't you got no manners ? There, take my trunk and carry out,—quick." The gentleman who was to take the charge of her on the journey home handed her into the stagecoach. She had not so much as thanked Mrs. Fanshaw and Zephina for their kindness and attention, but, as the coach was about to drive off, she gave them a sort of supercilious, condescending bow, as much as to say, " I have done you great honor by staying a couple of months with you, in your humble cottage."

" O, would some power the giftie gie us,
To see oursel's as others see us,
It would from many a folly free us,
And foolish notion."

LETTER FROM HARRIET ANN TO ZEPHINA.

Soon after Harriet Ann left Baxter, she addressed the following letter to Zephina, which, as it was never answered, was the only one with which she was *afflicted.*

" New York, August 28th.

" Deer Zephina : —

" I told you I would let you know how I got

home, so I write to let you know I got home *safe*, but very *mutch fatuged.*

"I found pa was n't very well; but between you and I and the post, I do n't think he is sick,—only cross and low-spirited. I *teezed* him till he let me go to dancing-school, which I *begun* last *Teusday.* I am going to learn to *gallophard* and to *walts*, and after a while to learn the *Mazoorker.* You know I can dance Spanish dances and *cotilyons* very well now; but, as I am *deturmined* to be a complete lady, you know I must learn all these things *purfectly.*

"O, do you know I have got the sweetest *Parris* bonnet! It is a *purfect* little love, and cost fifteen dollars. Pa scolded and scolded about it, because he said it was *ecstravvagunt* for a thin summer bonnet; but it is the most *becomeing* thing you ever *see*, and no body that is any body wears an American bonnet now-a-days.

"Can't think how you content yourself in the country with those common folks, the Morrises. For my part, I was delighted to get back to the *citty*, though a great many folks are so silly that they are now in the country. I have got to go and practice, so I can't write any more at present From your *affecsionate freind*,

"HARRIETTA ANNA."

Bad spelling is so common among young girls, that they scarcely consider it vulgar; yet nothing more completely stamps an ill-educated person. A letter, however fine the composition and writing may be, is vulgar if misspelt. Ungrammatical expressions, too, like those of Harriet Ann, are quite too frequently heard. And, besides these, that thick, inarticulate enunciation, and what is called clipping of words, is often spoken of as a marked peculiarity in Americans who style themselves ladies. There is a French proverb, "You know a lady when she opens her mouth"; and it is as true here as in France. It is very easy to discover a well-bred girl by her good grammatical English, well pronounced and distinctly enunciated.

CHAPTER VIII.

THE BOWER.

By the old oak-tree, Beulah, with the aid of Medad, built a rustic bower. To be sure it was only made of long hoop-poles, bent into a circular form and fastened into the ground; but flowering-beans, morning-glories, and honeysuckles, planted there by Beulah, soon covered it with a graceful drapery of leaves and flowers.

Medad placed a rude bench within the bower, upon which the girls often sat for an hour in the morning, in social chat, and, lest it should be damp for their feet, he had paved it with white pebbles. In one corner was a box marked "P. O.," in which frequent letters were deposited; and often, too, the little basket was there filled with delicacies, which Zephina carried home and shared with her mother.

Not far from the bower, a sweet little silvery brook merrily danced along over the smooth pebbles, from whose green margin the speckled trout darted forth and then retreated. Arm in arm, the girls often followed its meandering course, to the place where it fell over the rocks, in a sparkling little cascade, and then returned through a beautiful grove near by.

Every day some new beauty was added to the beloved bower. Beulah brought the most precious flowers from her garden and placed them there, and Zephina transplanted wild flowers from the woods, which bloomed sweetly beside their foreign companions. She printed in large capitals, "SACRED TO FRIENDSHIP," and placed it directly in front, and it lasted till — the first heavy rain!

It was one of the loveliest days in September, and Mrs. Fanshaw had given Zephina the privilege of passing the whole afternoon in the bower. Beulah had brought out a little table and tea-apparatus, and they were to take tea there, and talk over their past lives, — for up to this time Zephina had never mentioned her former place of residence. They had gathered wild flowers and evergreens, to tie into wreaths to hang up in fes toons about the bower, and while thus employed Zephina began her story.

"Once there was a girl who lived in New York. Is n't that the way that all children begin a story? Can you believe it, Beulah, I never went out of the bounds of the city, till I was twelve years old; all beyond it was in the *Miz*."

"Where is that?" asked Beulah.

"You know in the fourth commandment it says, 'in heaven and earth, the sea, and all *that in them is*.' When I was a mere child I understood it, 'and *all that 's in the Miz*'; and, O, how many conjectures I made about that queer place. All the dwarfs, giants, and fairies that I read about, and all the odd creations of my own imagination, the funniest things, all lived in the Miz. Now when I think of it, I do believe that all that was not New York was to me in the Miz. In the nursery the first trouble that I remember was an eating-apron."

"What do you mean by an eating-apron, dear; one that was only worn to eat in?" asked Beulah.

"Exactly so; a tier, pinafore, or whatever you choose to call it, that I was obliged to get for myself and put on, before I could eat any thing.

Then I might spill and daub as much as I pleased, if my dress was only safe. I exclaimed then, 'An eating-apron is the plague of my life!' and I have often thought so since, for I never learned to eat carefully and neatly; to this day, as you may have noticed, my dresses are covered with spots. If it had n't been for those plagues of eating-aprons, I should have learned to carry my food safely to my mouth, without poking my head clear over my plate."

"I think you might, Zephina," said Beulah, "for I have worn white aprons ever since I can remember, and my mother never let me have on more than three a week. If I soiled them, I was obliged to wear them for a punishment. Only see, I wear them now, at thirteen, just as I did when I was a very little girl; but I can keep one clean a whole week — unless I tie wreaths," said she, smiling to see how she had already soiled the snow-white apron.

"Well, I must have been a real torment in the nursery," continued Zephina; "for I took no care at all of my clothes; and when they were off, either left them scattered about for the nurse to pick up, or kicked them into a heap, which habit, I am sorry to say, I have but just left off. Another naughty trick that I learned in the nursery was, to eat as fast as I could, and all that was sent to me. Even now, I never look out for any body but myself at table.

"You would have laughed, Beulah, to see me eat up the soft milk-toast provided for an invalid gentleman where we were visiting. I did not observe that it was made on purpose for him, and placed in a little covered dish by the side of his plate. When he lifted the cover, I looked so lovingly at the toast, that the kind old gentleman offered me a piece. I took it, and finding it very nice, helped myself till the dish was entirely empty, and the poor sick man, who had eaten but half a slice, looked at me with a grim kind of a smile and remarked, that I 'really had an uncommonly fine appetite.'

"Another time I went with mamma to take tea with a very rich old lady who did not attend parties, but only invited a friend now and then, as a great favor. She was a particular sort of a lady. Mamma had often told me that she was one of the most complete ladies of the old school. I used to wonder, by the way, whose school that was.

"At the tea-table, which was furnished with the richest silver and the most beautiful china that I had ever seen, I found the biscuits quite to my liking, though they were so small that I always called them stingy biscuits; so, every time they were handed round I took one, till at length mamma, quite mortified, said, 'Zephina, dear, you seem very fond of Mrs. Foote's delicious biscuits.' 'Why, mamma,' said I, 'they are very small, and I 've only eaten seven.'

"The look the lady gave me ought to have frightened me; but somehow it was so droll, that I was just ready to laugh; but, hoping the laugh would go down with some tea, I took a large swallow of it, but the laugh would come. I held my hand over my mouth, but the tea spattered between my fingers all over the table, while I coughed and strangled, dropped my cup, and broke both cup and saucer.

"I, who was to be educated for a lady from my very cradle, with such vulgar manners! Mamma's well-bred friend looked absolutely horror-struck. But do you know, Beulah, I never felt the importance of refined manners till since I have seen such an example of the want of them in Harriet Ann. Now I have resolved to break myself of those disgusting nursery habits.

"Another of my trials was to be dressed for

company. They put my hair into papers, for it was no more inclined to curl than a bunch of jack-straws; and, O, they did pull and hurt me unmercifully to get them out and in order, at a moment's warning, when I was called for in the drawing-room. I remember once being thus dressed, just like a miniature fine lady, and carried down to be shown to visiters. Some one proposed that I should be set upon a marble centre-table, and recite a piece of poetry. With the reward of a whole pound of candy which was promised me in a whisper, I undertook to recite Wordsworth's 'We are Seven.'

"No doubt I murdered that beautiful little piece. At any rate, there must have been a striking contrast between poor over-dressed me, and the 'simple child' with 'a rustic woodland air.' I do not know whether I thought of any such thing, then, or whether the sweet sentiment of the little girl who would insist they still were seven had touched my young heart. But, when the flatterers praised me to the skies, calling me the best little lady in the world, I burst into passionate crying, and said, 'I am not a good little lady. I 'm the naughtiest little girl that ever was.' Then I was dismissed in disgrace to the nursery, and the pound of candy that I had fairly earned was unjustly refused to my entreaty. But poor mamma must be excused, for she was a very fashionable lady, and meant that I, her only daughter, should become very accomplished. Do n't you pity me, Beulah, for all these troubles ? "

" I do, indeed ; but yet I think, Zephina, you ought to have been more anxious to please your mother."

" I was anxious to please her, but then I never took the right way. I believe I was born for the country, for I have a natural love of it, and I never cared for the balls, concerts, theatres, and parties, to which mamma always took me. Then I hated flattery, because I had a genuine love of truth. I do not remember ever to have told but one falsehood in my life, and of that I am even at this time so much ashamed, I can't bear to think of it. When I was about ten years old, the gentlemen who visited at our house talked to me a great deal, and I answered them with simple truth, in such a way, often, as to give offence ; and mamma scolded me, telling me I was dreadfully impolite.

" I remember once, in particular, a gentleman

praised my beautiful natural curls, as he called them, and, soon after, asked me if I did not like him. 'No, Sir, I do not like you,' I answered. 'Why not?' he asked, in the most coaxing tone. 'Because, Sir, you do not tell the truth.' 'That is a great accusation for a little lady to make. What have I said that was untrue?' he inquired. I told him he knew very well that my curls were not natural, for they had just been taken out of papers, and were as stiff as wires. He laughed heartily, telling me that I would never do for a fashionable lady, — I was altogether too honest.

"Sitting up late at night made me pale and sickly, and I do not believe I should have lived till this time, if it had not been for this dear Baxter, and the comfort I have taken here."

"But, Zephina, did you never have any playthings?" said Beulah. "When I was a child, I can't remember that I ever did any thing but play. Medad and I used to build cob-houses in the garret, and slide down on the hay in the barn, and I had rag-babies, that I dressed and undressed, made their clothes, and washed and ironed them. We used to build bridges over the brooks, and, in winter, make great snowball houses, and go coasting down the hills, and sliding on the ice. And I have always had my garden and my flowers."

"O, delightful!" exclaimed Zephina, "how you must have enjoyed yourself! But I never was a child, — never. You need not smile, Beulah; you think I am childish enough now; — but I mean, I never had any such joyous childhood as you describe.

"I had two great wax-dolls, beautifully dressed; but I was not allowed to play with them. O, no; one was to walk out with in Broadway. She was dressed in the height of the fashion by the mantuamaker, and always had a new bonnet every time I had one, exactly like mine; I called her Miss Prim. The other was in full dress, blue satin with a lace over-dress. I had to carry her into the drawing-room, and was taught to hold her very gracefully. She was Miss Prue. I almost hated both of them, and used to cry because Miss Prim was so heavy that it really tired my arm to carry her, while nurse dragged me along by the other. So, one day when I was alone, I smashed in Prim's nose, picked out Prue's eyes, and cut off every silken curl from their doll-ships' heads, and there was an end of dolls for me. I was n't allowed to use a needle much, for fear it would spoil my fingers; no wonder it invented all kinds of mischief.

"But, Beulah, dear, I did have one darling pet, the sweetest little lapdog, with a blue ribbon round his neck; I loved him dearly, but he sometimes would soil his little feet, and then he would jump upon me, and spoil my dresses, or I would take him up when a big dog was coming along and carry him, and mamma was obliged to give him away, and I cried for weeks, and I can't think of him now — the little darling — without being just ready to cry.

"But see, Beulah, what a long wreath I 've made, and yours is longer yet. Let us fasten them up, and then you must tell your story. There, now, they look beautifully, it really is like a fairy palace. We must make one more wreath just to go round our motto. Come, Beulah, go on with your history."

"I have very little to tell. You know I have always lived in the country, and have never been to any place larger than Perkinsville, ten miles off. Of course I love the country and my own plain, kind family. One of the first things that I remember distinctly is my great love for sister

Eunice. She was the oldest of the family, and so good and so beautiful that she seemed to me different entirely from all other human beings. Is n't it strange? She has been gone ever since I was six years old, and yet I remember her perfectly, and her sweet smile often comes before me when I am asleep and when I am awake."

"And where has she gone?" asked Zephina, with surprise.

"To heaven," solemnly replied Beulah. "She died; and they told me she was going to heaven to be an angel. I went into the room where she was laid out, so pure and white, with her long hair loose, and still in its natural ringlets. I put my hand upon her icy forehead; I think I feel the chill now it was so dreadful. Then I sat down by her side and waited, for I expected to see her go away with angel's wings, as I had seen them in the great Bible. There I sang the little hymns she had taught me, for in my childishness I thought it would comfort her, and one of the hymns happened to be the one beginning

'Vital spark of heavenly flame,
Quit, O, quit this mortal frame.'

I was singing this, when my mother found me

there, and she called my father to listen, and never shall I forget how they cried and sobbed, as if their hearts were breaking. I told them what I was waiting for, and they drew me away, telling me that my sister's spirit would go to heaven, but that her beautiful corpse must be laid in the cold grave. It was the first time that I had heard of the grave, and it made me very sorrowful for a long time that my sweet sister should be covered up in that dark place.

"The way in which I was finally comforted may seem to you strange, Zephina. One evening I had stayed longer than usual in the front-yard. I had always been to bed at or before sundown. That evening I discovered something very wonderful in the clear western sky, and asked, 'What is that? What is that bright thing far away there, over the tops of the trees?' 'Why, child, it is a star; did you never see a star before?' 'No, mother; I never heard of such a thing. Did you ever see it before?' She told me that was the evening star, but that the whole sky was brilliant with stars every clear night. 'And do they never come down to the ground?' 'No; they always stay in the same place in the heavens.'

"I went to bed, but not to sleep. As soon as it was dark, I got up and opened the window-shutter, and looked out, and there were those beautiful stars shining in the sky, — and there my sister has gone, I thought; — there she still lives, — somewhere far off among those bright stars, — and in some mysterious way she has passed through the dark grave to reach them, — and I was comforted. And, Zephina, ever since, I love the stars with a solemn kind of joy that I can't describe. And when I told my mother, she said, 'We know that the dead shall rise again to immortal life, because our blessed Saviour rose from the grave, and ascended to heaven.' And she read me all about the Saviour in the great Bible, and I have loved that holy book ever since, and read it more than any other."

There was a pause of a few moments; — then Zephina, with eyes full of tears, said, "Well, you are a dear, good little soul, as pure as those white lilies."

"O, no Zephina, I am not; you do n't know how hard I find it to be good. There is scarcely a day passes that I do n't commit some fault for which I am sorry."

"Well, nobody sees them but yourself," replied her partial friend.

"You forget, dear Zephina, there is one who sees all evil things in our hearts."

"I have forgotten this too long," was the sincere reply; "but I am sorry, and shall try to be a better girl, especially to my mother."

They suspended the wreath around the motto, and then they put the tea-kettle on a little furnace, that Medad had built near the bower; and some short sticks of wood were there, and some coals nicely covered over with ashes. Soon they had a bright fire. And they spread their table with a white napkin, and placed upon it cake, biscuits, and sweetmeats. And, when the tea was ready, they made a signal for Medad by clapping their hands; — and he came, but there was no seat for him, and he was so tall that his head touched the top of the bower, and Zephina told him he must kneel, for that was the way that knights errant of olden time did in the presence of ladies. Never was a repast more enjoyed than that in the bower "Sacred to Friendship."

CHAPTER IX.

PARTING TOKENS.

The pure enjoyments of that rude bower and its post-office, — what in after life could equal them! But as all earthly things, however sweet and beautiful, must fade and die, a frost, "a killing frost," came early in the autumn, and the shrivelled leaves could no longer conceal the rude framework. Medad, fruitful in expedients, cut down branches of evergreen, with which he covered it, but soon the snow came and blocked it up and the poor bower was deserted. But then there were winter amusements. There was a large pond frozen over, and Medad was a fine skater. And his sled was arranged so that the two girls could sit upon it. Warmly wrapped in their cloaks, he drew them swiftly over the smooth surface. And, when summer fruits were gone, there were still plenty of nuts and apples for Zephina.

After the visit of Mrs. Whately, Mrs. Fanshaw was quite reconciled to Zephina's intimacy with Beulah, and gave her every facility for cultivating it, though she never repealed the law that forbade her daughter to go into the farm-house. She was herself occupied continually with her worsted-work, and silk patchwork. Day after day she bent over the embroidery-frame, bringing out, by slow degrees, "Sir Walter Scott and his Family," as a mate to "The Interior of a Dutch Inn," for a pair of ottomans.

Winter passed rapidly away, and spring once more smiled upon the reviving earth. The bower had been nicely cleared out and put in order, and warning given to Zephina that the post-office was again opened. Zephina appeared there soon after, at a very early hour in the morning. She sat down upon the rude bench, and, leaning an elbow on her knees covered her face with one hand; in the other was the little basket that had so often been filled with gifts from her beloved friend.

The large tears trickled through her fingers and fell upon it. After a short time spent thus she rose, and, placing it upon the bench, said, "Dear little basket! shall I never see you again? Would that I could fill you with gold, — but that would be a poor return for my sweet Beulah's kindness." Then, giving one more longing, lingering look at the bower, and at the dear old oak, she walked rapidly away.

Beulah soon arrived there, and, seeing Zephina in the distance, called her, but she was beyond the reach of her voice. She took up the basket; it was full. A letter was upon the top of it; it was as follows: —

"'I cannot but hope that I shall meet my dearest friend to-morrow morning, — yet I may not; and then, — how shall I write it? — and then, we may never meet again.

"Mamma has decided to go immediately to the city, to 'finish my education.' Poor, dear mamma, she is not very well, and I have not said a word in opposition to it, though I am sure it is not in my nature to be such a lady as she wishes me to be. 'I go for comfort,' as the dear, dear Squire says. In the basket you will find a worsted comforter that I have knitted for him; when he wears it, next winter, may it remind him of the little girl to whom he was so kind. The work-bag is for your mother; give it to her, with my sincere regards. The pen-wiper is for Mr. Azariah; I am not certain, however, that he writes much. The watch-case is for Mr. Medad. The flower upon it is a forget-me-not; — do not tell him, however, for I do n't believe he would know but what it is a turnip-blossom, for I embroidered it without any pattern. For you, my sweet Beulah, I have nothing but a heart full of love, and that poor little book-mark, done with my own hair; if you could see to the bottom of that heart, you would find 'Gratitude' as plainly there as it is upon the mark. Put it in your Bible, that very Bible I have so often seen you carry to Sunday School, that you may be in the most solemn manner re ninded of the enduring affection of

"ZEPHINA."

CHAPTER X.

A GENTLE REPROOF.

Beulah was sad and lonely for some time after the departure of her friend. But she was a busy little body, and constant occupation soon brought back her cheerfulness. She received a box of books and a new bonnet and dress from Mrs. Whately, which the Squire said he was mightily afraid would turn her head. But she kept it as steadily when at church as ever, and every Sunday went for a poor blind woman, as usual, whom she led carefully to her seat near the pulpit, and, as soon as church was over led her home again. She soon wrote to her kind friend the following letter.

"My dear Mrs. Whately: —

"I thank you a thousand times for your kind

letter and acceptable presents. The books I am reading with pleasure. I like Miss Edgeworth's stories very much indeed. The last that I read was Mademoiselle Panache. I suppose Lady Caroline was of the kind of fine ladies that my dear Zephina dislikes so much. They have gone from Baxter, — Mrs. Fanshaw and her daughter, — and I do not even know where they are now living. I suppose it was forbidden to Zephina to tell me the place of their residence. Instead of her pleasant society I am sometimes troubled with the visits of a young man who is studying medicine in our village. He is known by every person here as 'the Doctor's young man.'

"Now this Dr. Weasenby has taken it into his head to pay us a weekly visit. He is queer looking, — very. His hair is light and long, and in front it stands up straight and stiff; — he must use quantities of pomatum. His large, light-grey eyes *seem* to stare at you, and yet he never looks directly in the face of any one. Then he holds his head so stiffly on his long neck, which collars and cravats can't cover. But, to crown the whole, this awkward gawky thinks himself so handsome and so polite, — he is such a conceited fellow, — that I am troubled to know how to treat him civilly. What shall I do, my dear Mrs. Whately? He comes every Thursday night, when mother has gone to the sewing-circle, and father has just received the Weekly Advertiser. Medad goes to wait upon some of the girls home, and I have my suspicions that Azariah goes a courting.

"Dr. Weasenby says, 'Miss Morris,' (for he seems to take me for a young lady, instead of a little girl only fourteen,) Miss Morris, did you ever read the Life of Benjamin Franklin?' 'Yes, Sir, I have read *a* Life of Dr. Franklin.' 'Well, it 's a fine book, now, is n't it? Did you ever read Lord Byron?' 'Never.' 'Well, now, it 's a pity;—Lord Byron 's a pretty book; there 's some nice females in it that I should like to talk to you about. In the Corsair and the Bride of 'Bydos, them must have been uncommon handsome females.

"Then comes a long pause,—Father keeps on reading his paper,—the Doctor smooths up his hair in front and down behind,—I am very much engaged with my knitting. And thus he comes, week after week. The only change in his conversation of any consequence is, 'Did you ever read the Life of Washington?' or, 'Did you ever read

Josephus? It would be a grand book if it was n't so dreadful long that no man alive ever did get through it.'

"How shall I treat him? How can I be polite to such an awkward, stupid man? Please tell me, my dear friend, and much oblige your grateful and attached

"BEULAH."

The following reply was soon received.

"MY DEAR YOUNG FRIEND: —

"I fear in your last letter you indulged yourself a little in drawing a caricature. The poor, awkward young man seems quite harmless and inoffensive. Be kindly considerate towards him, if he is only homely and awkward. Think how much better this is, than if he were immoral or vicious. To be sure, it is sometimes difficult to refrain from laughter when things are really ridiculous, but as long as they are only ludicrous, in the manner you have mentioned, arising doubtless from the want of education and association with well-bred people, we ought to endure them with perfect good-nature.

"Be civil to the young man, Beulah, because your own self-respect demands it; be civil to every one, even to the lowest person whom you meet. Besides, you might yourself fall into the society of people accustomed to elegant manners, who would see some things in you, that, if so disposed, they might ridicule. I have often seen clusters of young ladies in a party, making sport of every body. No person, however good or dignified, could escape. Any little peculiarity of dress, gait, or expression, they would seize upon, and show it up in the most ludicrous manner. I have sometimes said, in passing such a lively group, 'Well, girls, who now are you dissecting? I fear I shall be your next victim.'

"I know, my dear Beulah, the kindness of your heart, and do not believe you would ever thus amuse yourself in society. Those who are guilty would say it is only thoughtlessness, — but I think there is some maliciousness in it, too.

"Another habit that girls fall into is that of giggling continually. They cannot speak without a titter or a giggle. This not only looks very silly, but it destroys the quiet self-possession that becomes a young lady.

"Some girls, too, bite their handkerchiefs or gloves, or worse yet their nails; this last is an odious habit. They ought to learn to keep their hands laid gently and easily together when they are sitting; in this way they will in time acquire a lady-like repose, essential to female dignity.

"Do not grow weary, my Beulah, with your friend, because she thus tells you freely how to cultivate good manners. I know that you have the requisite foundation, and all in good time the superstructure will be reared. You will, in short, become all that my most sanguine wishes could desire. God bless you, dearest.

"Your true friend,

'LAURA WHATELY.

CHAPTER XI.

AN UNEXPECTED INVITATION.

BEULAH had grown in beauty and in gracefulness from year to year. The native sweetness of her disposition had not been embittered by unkindness; neither had her self-respect been decreased by comparing herself with those above her in rank and fortune. Was not Squire Morris a justice of the peace, a substantial farmer, a man of consequence in the town of Baxter? She had never experienced an emotion of self-degradation, nor wished to degrade others. Why should she?

At fourteen, her slender figure alarmed her mother, lest she should have a feeble constitution, yet the fine air of the country and active exercise gave her complexion a rosy hue, without injuring its delicacy, and the vigor and elasticity of her movements proved that she was in perfect health.

In the autumn, the Squire received a long letter from Mrs. Whately, mentioning various reasons why she wished Beulah to come and pass a year with her. These reasons did not transpire, for the careful man, having the old-fashioned notion, that a woman cannot keep a secret, did not read the letter even to Mrs. Morris.

It was exceedingly trying to the whole family to part with the lamb of the flock. Beulah herself was at first unwilling to leave home. Where else could she be so happy? And how could mother do without her?

But then Mrs. Whately was so kind, — so very kind, — and she was lonely, too, and a comfort she might be to her, — and there were a great many things in the world that she would like to see and hear, — and, with the hopefulness and vivacity of youth, she looked forward to the time when she should return and tell so many things to the loved ones at home.

Three whole days were spent by Mrs. Morris and Beulah in preparations for the city, and her simple wardrobe was considered in complete order.

How it would have amused a girl of her age, accustomed to think of dress as the most important thing in the world, to see the simple attire with which Beulah Morris felt perfectly satisfied.

Beulah took an affectionate leave of every body in the village, for she knew every man, woman, and child, and was a favorite with all. She lingered long at the beloved bower, which with girlish fondness she still kept in order for the sake of Zephina.

"Medad," said the Squire, "you must go with Beulah, and take good care of her, and you may spend two or three days in Boston and see what 's to be seen."

"I am delighted, perfectly delighted, with the chance," said Medad, — and he whispered something in the ear of Beulah. "But shall we go in our waggon?" continued he

"No, no; take to stages and railroads, and start to-morrow," replied Squire Morris. "And, Beulah, although cousin Whately is very kind to you, I do n't want you to feel at all dependent upon her, for I 'm too thankful to say that I am well to do in the world and need n't ask favors of any one. You go to do her a favor by staying and keeping her company in her lonely house. And here is one hundred dollars for your spending money. That will keep you as well dressed for the year as a farmer's daughter ought to be ; for I do n't want to have you get any grand notions in your head, and come home to despise your father and mother, because they do n't care for show and only go for comfort. Be friendly with every one, but by no means too familiar. Remember the old proverb, — Familiarity breeds contempt."

The tears were in Beulah's mild eyes.

"O, do n't cry my child, I know you 'll be a good, sensible Yankee girl, and not be carried away by all the novelties you chance to meet. Your grandmother was a good woman, not to say any thing of your mother, because praise to the face is open disgrace ; at any rate, you come of a good stock, and you must keep up its character."

CHAPTER XII.

THE JOURNEY.

EARLY in the morning, the stagecoach, with its nine inside passengers and three outsides, was on the route to Boston. For several miles Beulah did not lower her handkerchief from her eyes, excepting once, and that was to catch a glimpse of their own dear village from the last high hill. Home! home! and the kind warm hearts there, what in the wide world could atone for their loss.

"Come, cheer up, Beulah," said Medad; "our folks, though they did feel sadly, will be chirk again soon. And there are a great many pleasant things to be seen on the way."

Medad's kind intentions towards his sister were aided by a sudden jolt, which sent a gentleman's hat directly into her face.

"I beg your pardon, Miss," said the owner of the hat, a young gentleman who sat directly opposite to Beulah.

"Not at all, Sir," the words were, of course. but the tone of voice made the stranger desire to hear it again. But there was something in the air and manner of the simply dressed country-girl before him, that prevented him from addressing her. Several times he was upon the point of doing so, but he could not. At length he turned to Medad, and said, "A very fine country this. It is better, however, for grazing than for grain, I should think."

"Perfectly correct, Sir," replied Medad; "it 's a fine grass country; they say it 's much better land, though, in that famous valley of the Connecticut."

"The valley of the Connecticut is very beautiful; — its banks are quite a contrast to the bold banks of the Hudson. Have you ever been up the Hudson?"

"Never, Sir," said Medad; "never was twenty miles from Baxter in my life."

The stranger looked a little surprised at this frank avowal, but Medad was utterly unconscious of having said any thing remarkable. He did not consider it in the slightest degree disgraceful not to have travelled. Why should he?

Next to Beulah, on the middle seat, was a coarse-looking woman, who seemed disposed to be incommoded, for the slightest cause was made a matter of petulant complaint. The back-strap wanted fixing, — somebody's feet were in her way, — at last she began to be sick with riding. Beulah politely offered her the seat by the window, which she accepted. Then she opened her travelling-wallet, and handed the woman a bottle of camphor, and some peppermint lozenges, with which her careful mother had provided her. The woman accepted them, without a word of thanks.

They had not gone more than twenty miles, before a disaster occurred. They were about passing a small bridge. The horses went safely over, but the heavily-laden coach was upon the bridge when one side of it gave away, and the coach was upset. Fortunately the bridge was low, and over a shallow stream. The outside passengers were precipitated into the water. The driver sprang from his seat to the ground, and kept hold of the reins.

Inside were dire confusion and intense alarm. The petulant woman screamed, and struggled, and kicked, endangering the life and limbs of her neighbours more than the fall had done. As soon as possible, the driver cut the traces, and, securing the horses by the road-side, came to the assistance of the passengers. The outsides by this time had discovered that they were still alive and not much injured, and aided the driver in relieving the other passengers from the "durance vile" in which they were still kept within the coach.

Medad was the first to make his way out. The young gentleman followed. "Now help Beulah," said the former.

"No," said her sweet voice within; "help this poor woman, who has been very much injured. Let me assist you to rise."

By this time all were out excepting these two, — and it seemed impossible to do any thing with the woman, who had entirely lost all command of herself. "O, my arm! O, my arm! The weight of the whole load came right on me," she screamed.

With the aid of Beulah within, and the passengers without, she was at length dragged out of the coach and placed upon *terra-firma.*

Beulah could have escaped uninjured only

by being on the middle seat; she was thus thrown upon her unfortunate neighbour. The poor woman was shivering with cold from her wet clothing. Beulah took off her own shawl and wrapped it about her, for her arm was dreadfully bruised and broken. No sooner had she done so, than a short broadcloth cloak was thrown around her own shoulders by the young gentleman.

"Where do you belong, my good woman?" said Medad.

"About five miles from here," she replied; "but I shall never live to get there."

"O, yes, you will, for the driver has sent a man on horseback for another coach, and it 's only a mile. Is n't it lucky that we were only one mile from the place where they change horses? — and they have an extra stage there. And soon you 'll be home, and the doctor will set your arm in less than no time. It will be as strong as ever it was in a month."

"O, I never shall have the use of it again," she said; "I am always worse off than any body in the world."

The young gentleman had succeeded in getting into the coach, and had brought out some cushions and Beulah's wallet. She took off the poor woman's bonnet, wiped off the water, bent it into shape, and put it again upon her head, quite forgetful of her own, until Medad said, "You look funny enough, Beulah, with your own bonnet knocked into a cocked hat, and that military cloak to correspond."

All the passengers who were not disabled went to work to place the luggage upon the shore, ready for the coach. They had just got it all there when it arrived, and soon they were surprised to find themselves again on their way with so little injury. Bruises and scratches there were in abundance, but no limbs broken but the woman's arm. They all agreed to go on immediately to the place where she belonged, instead of stopping at the next inn to make themselves more comfortable, for she seemed in great pain and distress. Beulah wished to support her head upon her shoulder, but the young gentleman insisted upon relieving her from the burden.

In less than an hour the coach stopped at the inn. Medad and the stranger, finding that it was a quarter of a mile from the main road to the woman's home, took a waggon and carried her there. So much delay had been occasioned, that they all concluded that it was best to remain there for the night.

The shawl was safely returned to Beulah by the young gentleman, who, with some hesitation, delivered the message. As, however, it showed some gratitude, though expressed in her own coarse manner, he thought it his duty to do so. "She said to me, 'Tell that girl who lent me the shawl that she deserves the best husband in the world, and I hope when she 's old enough she 'll find him.'"

Beulah blushed, and said, in a very low tone, "I am much obliged to her."

The next day's journey was without accident. And then, by railroad, they came to their place of destination.

"Look out, Beulah,—there is Bunker Hill Monument," said Medad; "so our friend says. Does n't it make one's blood start through the veins to see it. And old Boston, too, the Cradle of American Liberty."

CHAPTER XIII.

CITY ACQUAINTANCES.

MRS. WHATELY was expecting her young friends and received them with the greatest cordiality. Her house was large, and situated in one of the finest streets in Boston. Medad looked at the various articles of rich furniture with wondering eyes. The first opportunity that Beulah had to see him alone was after dinner. She begged him not to gaze about quite so much, and by no means to ask any questions.

"That is too good, Beulah, advising me just as if you had always lived in the city," said Medad, laughing. "And I should have thought really you had, by the way you dipped your fingers into those colored glasses and wiped them on the napkin; for my part, I could n't think what they were for, and should just as likely have taken a drink, if I had n't see you go through with the operation. And then, that fork with four prongs bothered me, — but you handled it as if you never had used any thing but a silver fork in your life."

"It only needs a little observation to be able to change in these small things from what we have been accustomed to at home," said Beulah. 'What beautiful pictures these are."

"Yes; they are, and this is a fine house, but our folks could buy house and all, if they wanted it," replied Medad, walking to and fro in the splendid apartment, without the least consciousness of inferiority, because he had not always trodden upon a Wilton carpet. Medad was one who

> "Would shake hands with a king upon his throne,
> And think it kindness to his Majesty."

The next day, Mrs. Whately, not being well, was unable to go out with Medad and Beulah. She gave them very particular directions that they need not loose their way amid the intricacies of Boston, a perfect labyrinth to strangers, and they started for a stroll in Washington Street.

Medad, entirely satisfied with his suit of butternut-brown, made by the country tailor, walked leisurely along, looking in at the shop windows. At length he stopped before one, saying, "What beautiful trinkets, and splendid watches! Come, Beulah, let us go in here."

"If you wish to make a purchase, I will go in with you, but not otherwise," replied Beulah.

But Medad, without replying, was already within. He inquired the price of their watches, and the man carelessly answered, "Some are two hundred and some three hundred."

"Well, Sir, but have n't you any for less than that. I want a good time-piece, — a plain, good one, suitable for a farmer," said Medad. "There 's one, now, what 's the price of that?"

"Fifty dollars."

Medad looked at it awhile, and then whispered to his sister, "Do you think that would fit *the* watch-case?"

"I should think it would, exactly," she answered.

"Then that 's the watch for me. I 'll take it, Sir, if you 'll put a key to it." And he handed out fifty dollars. He had been laying it by for some time, to be able to fill the beloved watch case.

They then sauntered along, Medad making his

remarks upon all whom they met in an under tone to Beulah.

"There, now, what do you call that walk, — that girl coming towards us with the yellow bonnet and red feather flying off half a yard, and all those curls. I should call it the diddlecum-twiddle. Did you ever see such a jerking and twitching to make progress forward?"

Beulah looked at the girl with the long, light curls hanging down each side to her waist, and as she did so they were quite near her. Medad began bowing and smiling. The girl raised her eye-glass, and, looking at him through it, said to her companion, in the most affected tone, "What microscopic insect is that? I am cer tain I never saw it before."

"Miss Harriet Ann Gunn, I believe," said Medad, perfectly undaunted. "Can you tell me what has become of Miss Zephina Fanshaw?"

"I do not know any such person," said the girl, hurrying on with all her might.

"You must be mistaken," said Beulah. "That could not be Harriet Ann."

"Mistaken! I should know her among ten thousand. How provoking that she should tell such a falsehood! Fine feathers, it seems, do n't always make fine birds. Keep a look out, — we may meet Zephina. Do you suppose she, too, would n't know us?"

"I do n't know, indeed, for I am told that people here often forget those they have known in the country, — but I do not believe Zephina would ever forget old friends."

When Beulah related this little adventure to Mrs. Whately, the good lady was quite amused to find that her young friends had never heard of "cutting an acquaintance." She told them it was a vulgar practice that some persons had who must be very doubtful of their own respectability, since it depended entirely upon that of their acquaintances.

"You may rely upon it," said she, "that no one cuts an acquaintance, who is perfectly contented with her position in the world. She has no reason to do so, for if the person she chances to meet is above her, she bows with respect, and without envy; if below, still with politeness, and without a condescending, patronizing air. It is therefore more than probable that this girl would not be a suitable acquaintance for us."

After passing a few days in Boston, and seeing much that was worthy of a stranger's notice, Medad was anxious to know how the watch would fit the case, and, telling Beulah, "Our folks will be anxious to hear from us by this time," he bade her an affectionate farewell, charging her to keep a bright look-out for Zephina.

CHAPTER XIV.

SHOPPING.

Mrs. Whately took Beulah out to make some needful purchases. No sooner did they enter a shop than the clerks were all politeness and attention. It was not *altogether* because that lady came in her own carriage, but because there was in her mode of shopping something so agreeable that every one was pleased to wait upon her. She knew before she left home just what she wanted, and about what would be a reasonable price, and therefore never stood cheapening for hours the articles she intended to purchase.

She consulted Beulah's taste, for, like most girls, she had a taste of her own, and found that she invariably preferred the least glaring colors and the most simple style. As this entirely agreed with her own taste, it was not difficult to make a selection. After their return home, Mrs. Whately handed Beulah a little memorandum-book, saying, "It will be well for you to keep an account of your expenditures while absent from home. I have arranged it for you. You will find, among other things, a place to put down the pieces that you give to the chamber-maid for the washer-woman. Although I believe all my domestics to be honest, it is right that you should know certainly that every piece is returned. Habits of order and economy are important to every woman, rich or poor. In our country, especially, she who is rich to-day may be poor to-morrow; — and, besides, wealth should be expended conscientiously and with good taste."

"But," said Beulah, "I think those young ladies we met shopping to-day could not be very economical, for they wanted to purchase the greatest quantities of things, — lace, shawls, silks, velvets, every thing. The counters were heaped up with the various articles. And yet," said she, "they did try to be economical, for they asked again and again if that was the lowest price they could possibly take."

"They were probably only shopping for amusement. Many of them went home without purchasing a single article," said Mrs. Whately.

"How provoking it must be to the merchants," said Beulah. "I can't imagine what pleasure the young ladies take in such a strange amusement."

"I hope you never will know from experience," was the reply.

Beulah wrote in her little memorandum-book, with the greatest possible neatness, as follows:—

Received from my father, Oct. 15th, $ 100.00.

Expended:—

Cloak	$ 18.00
Bonnet	6.00
Gaiter-Boots and Shoes	3.50
Mousseline de Laine	6.50
Cravat	.50
Gloves	1.50
Handkerchiefs	3.00
Muff	6.00

"Forty-five dollars already!" exclaimed Beulah to herself, when she had added up her expenses; "I am afraid, at his rate, my hundred will not last through the year."

CHAPTER XV

A SURPRISE.

After Beulah had been in Boston about a month, she went one morning with Mrs. Whately to a milliner's in —— Street.

While Mrs. Whately was engaged making some purchases for herself, Beulah's attention was arrested by a familiar voice that she heard on the other side of the shop. She turned and looked. It was the voice of one of the young girls of the shop, waiting upon a customer. She looked again, and, approaching the girl, exclaimed, "Zephina!"

"Beulah Morris!" was the reply, and a warm embrace followed.

Mrs. Whately came towards them looking inquiringly. "It is Zephina, my own dear friend," said Beulah. "Mrs. Whately, Zephina."

"Is it possible?" exclaimed Mrs. Whately

shaking hands most cordially. "I congratulate you both on this unexpected meeting." But as this was not a suitable place for explanation, she asked Zephina to come and see Beulah very soon, and gave her address.

"I have but little time," she replied, looking very sorrowfully, "but I will endeavour to come as soon as possible."

Mrs. Whately and Beulah then left, and, all the way home, they were forming conjectures how Zephina had happened to take up the employment in which they found her engaged.

As they stepped out of the shop and into the carriage, Harriet Ann happened to be passing, and saw them.

"I declare, that is the sister of the horrid wretch that spoke to me the other day in Washington Street, and she is with Mrs. Whately, one of the very fust ladies in Boston."

The person to whom she spoke was the same who was with her on the former occasion. "It 's the very young lady who was with him; what a very pretty girl she is," she replied.

"How can you think so? She has n't a bit of an air, — and so plainly dressed, too, — not even a feather, when every body that can raises one of some kind or other. She 's a real country-girl. I can't think how she happens to be with Mrs. Whately. Seems to me I remember she got her living in the country by picking berries, or some such thing, but I am uncerting. I am going down this way, and must bid you good morning."

She walked a little way down the street, and then, turning, hastened back to the milliner's shop. For many months, Harriet Ann had not found it convenient to recognize Zephina, and whenever she passed her in the street, it was amusing to see the various expedients that she adopted for turning her head the other way. Now she ran up to her, saying, in a condescending manner, "How d' ye do, Zephina. What have you got altogether *allamode* and *recherchy* (Harriet Ann had got a smattering of French, which she pronounced horridly, and a passion for large words).

"I do not understand you, Miss Gunn," replied Zephina.

"O, I forgot, your present occupation is an insuperable preventative to your studying French. By the way, I thought I saw this morning, that very country-girl that I once or twice met, when I spent a couple of months at that horrid outlandish place in the country. Her name is Betsey or Patty Morris, I believe?"

"Beulah Morris. She is passing the winter with her cousin, Mrs. Whately," coolly replied Zephina.

"Then that countrified fellow must have been her brother, who had the impudence to address me in the street, and inquire after you."

"Was it the older or the younger brother?" asked Zephina, slightly blushing.

"I am sure I do n't know; it was a tall, awkward crichure, and I was scared to death for fear some one would see him speak to me in the street."

A lady now came and asked Zephina to step aside, — she wished to ask her a question. Mrs. Markham — that was the lady's name — was getting up a set of *tableaux*, and wanted some one for a Rowena. She was struck with the long flaxen curls and fair complexion of Harriet Ann, as a fine contrast for her dark-haired, dark-eyed friend, who was to personate Rebecca the Jewess. Zephina told her that Harriet Ann was a young lady of independent fortune, niece to Mr. Prium, the baker.

"A very respectable, honest man, I 've known

him these twenty years," the lady said, and asked for an introduction to her.

Harriet Ann was delighted beyond expression at this invitation.

As the *tableaux* were to be the next evening, Mrs. Markham offered to procure a dress for Miss Gunn. But no, Miss Gunn chose to provide her own dress, if the lady would tell her what it should be, as she had not the least idea who or what Rowena was. Mrs. Markham explained it, recommending that she should leave it to the good taste of Miss Fanshaw.

CHAPTER XVI.

A FRIENDLY VISIT.

THE next morning Beulah was agreeably surprised by a visit from Zephina. The greeting was equally cordial on both sides.

Zephina told Beulah, that, when they were in Baxter, her mother had retired into the country for economy's sake. They had formerly lived in New York. Her mother had been a widow since she herself was an infant. Their fortune, which had once been considerable, had been reduced, yet Mrs. Fanshaw determined to bring out Zephina as an accomplished lady.

On her return to New York, she lost nearly all that remained of her fortune by the failure of a bank. Zephina immediately determined to offer herself for some kind of employment, but her mother insisted that it should not be in New York, the scene of her former display. She therefore, through their milliner, procured a place in Boston, where she had now been for more than a year. Not long after their arrrival, Mrs. Fanshaw was seized with a spine complaint, which had confined her for some months entirely to her bed.

"Poor mamma! she did every thing in her power for me, yet I was often very refractory," said Zephina. "She is now so kind and so patient, that it grieves me to think of it. I am obliged to leave her alone a great deal. I hope, Beulah, you will come and see her sometimes. We live in a room — yes, one room — in a house No. 19 —— Street."

"I will come very soon," said Beulah; "but will she know me?"

"Yes, for I shall tell her you are coming, and we have no acquaintances here. But do n't tell her if you please where you are staying. Are you taking music lessons, Beulah?"

She was; — her cousin had kindly offered to instruct her. "You were my first teacher in music," said Beulah. "Do you remember the bower where you taught me so many songs?"

"O, those were the happiest days of my life," replied Zephina sorrowfully.

But the hour that she had begged was past, and she must take leave.

"Come often and see me," said Beulah.

"No, dearest, I cannot come. It would not do at all. You will move in such a different sphere, that it would only be a mortification to you to own me for an intimate friend, and it would pain me to be received in any other way."

"That is the first unkind thing that you ever said to me, Zephina. It makes no difference what spheres we move in; nothing can divide our hearts."

"The same simple, kind-hearted Beulah!" exclaimed her friend, throwing her arms around her neck. "I must have one more kiss, and I will love you as well as ever, but I really have no time for paying visits,—not a moment to spare from my employment and from poor mamma."

Harriet Ann was anxiously waiting for Zephina. Her splendid dress of white satin, with a transparent gauze over-dress, must be finished, and she was in agony for fear it would not be done. Then she needed a magnificent white veil. This she asked Zephina to lend her from the shop, which was promptly refused.

"Then I must run in debt for one," said Harriet Ann, "for I have n't a dollar left of my quarterly *income*."

CHAPTER XVII.

LES TABLEAUX VIVANTS.

"It is not my intention, Beulah, to take you often into society," said Mrs. Whately; "you are quite too young; moreover, it would withdraw your attention from your studies, but as you have never seen any *tableaux*, I am going to take you to Mrs. Markham's this evening."

"*Tableaux*, — do n't laugh at my ignorance, — I am entirely at a loss to guess what they are."

"I never laugh at ignorance of any kind, and this — with regard to an amusement — is a mere trifle. *Tableaux vivants* are living pictures; — but I shall tell you no more, lest it should impair your enjoyment of the evening. You will find your dress already prepared, and laid in your room."

Beulah flew to her room, and there lay a simple

white-muslin dress, with a blue sash. She took her purse, went down to Mrs. Whately, and, putting it into her hand, begged to her to pay for it. She refused at once, having designed it for a present.

"I am very much obliged to you," said Beulah, "but my father forbade me to accept presents."

"Did he? — that was so like his sturdy independence; — then I must deny myself the pleasure, and take out of your purse the ten dollars that the dress cost. I should have consulted you, my dear, only I wished to give you an agreeable surprise. I am sorry that I must submit to so unpleasant a necessity."

As Beulah looked in the glass, arrayed for the evening, did she not feel a consciousness of her own loveliness? That fact never transpired. Faces have blushed at beholding their own beauty, and it is possible that hers did; but she had never been told that she had any personal charms. She was not vain, and it is just possible that she had never made the discovery.

Mrs. Markham's rooms were filled with as many as could see the pictures, and a few more who tried very hard. Expectation was on tiptoe. The curtain at length arose.

The frame for the *tableaux* was gorgeously gilded, the vista and lights well arranged for effect. The first *tableaux* was magnificent. It was a scene from Kenilworth. Elizabeth, when she discovers Amy Robsart in the grotto, att'red as a nymph.

The next was Rebecca the Jewess, and Rowena. The scene was the one in which Rebecca presents the casket, and asks to see the face that had won Ivanhoe. No one could have been more completely Saxon than *the* Rowena, and the dress, and the lights, and the contrast with the dark Jewess, made her look very prettily; — but the moment that the curtain was lifted, Harriet Ann burst into a silly, girlish giggle, and entirely spoiled the picture. The passionate Rebecca was so angry that she would not attempt the scene again, and Mrs. Markham with difficulty concealed her displeasure.

"That must have been Harriet Ann Gunn," said Beulah to Mrs. Whately.

"Very probably it was, from her behaviour," was the reply.

Several other *tableaux* followed, and were completely successful, — delighting the young country-girl, whose love for the beautiful was so deep and true, that few persons present could have received more enjoyment.

Extempore *tableaux* followed. Mrs. Markham came to Beulah, and requested her to sit for Hope Leslie. She frankly confessed that she knew nothing of the character, and therefore could not express it. Others were suggested, but Beulah said she should act entirely out of character as any thing but a spectator, and begged to be excused.

At this moment a young gentleman came up, and asked an introduction. "My son, Hugh Markham, Miss Morris," said the lady.

It was her travelling companion on the way from Baxter.

Harriet Ann had just taken a seat by Beulah, determined to claim acquaintance. "This is quite a novelty to you, Miss Morris," said she, pertly, — "quite a novelty. You do n't get up such beautiful things in Baxter."

"They are quite new to me," replied Boulah, "and very pleasing."

"Then I am not mistaken; I should have known that voice among ten thousand," said Markham.

"It is mellifluous and significant, certingly," abruptly exclaimed Harriet Ann.

Markham, though annoyed by this strange speech, was amused at its absurdity. He made another attempt, however, to converse with Beulah. "Do you pass the winter in Boston, Miss Morris?"

"I do; I am making quite a long visit to Mrs. Whately," she replied.

"Are you, indeed!" exclaimed Harriet Ann. "I am infinitely glad of it, for I have an imperious desire to become acquainted with her. Do me the satisfaction to introduce me, will you, Beulah? I must call you so, for it seems so like old times. But is n't yours a very queer name? Do you like it?"

"It was my grandmother's name," was the brief reply.

"Well, I do n't think any body ought, by good rights, to be named after their grandmother, for names do get so old-fashioned. I hope now we 've met, that I shall see you often in company this winter."

"I am too young to go into society; my studies will occupy most of my time" said Beulah.

"What difference does that make. I go to school, and yet I shall go into company a great deal. I am studying Music, Drawing, French, Italian, History, Chemistry, Geometry, Painting, Dancing, Composition, and Moral Philosophy. What are you studying, Beulah? and where do you go to school? I go to the fust school in Boston. I wonder you do n't go there."

"Mrs Whately is so kind as to instruct me at home."

"Well, now, that is very odd; I should n't think she'd find time. But now you will remember to call me Harriet Ann, won't you."

"Excuse me, miss," said Markham, "but what is your surname."

"Gunn. It's a horrible name to pun upon; I could tell you fifty capital ones that have been made upon it."

Markham could think of but one, he wished earnestly that it would go off.

"Are you trying to think of one?" inquired Miss Gunn. "I've heard you were excruciatingly witty. If you can't make it out, our young country friend might help you, for I believe she is what Yankees her way call smart."

"I never made a pun in my life," said Beulah.

"Well, it is strange how little of *bagatelle* people up country do know," said Miss Gunn.

Beulah's quiet smile was unperceived by Harriet Ann, but did not escape the notice of Markham.

"How do you like my costume?" inquired Harriet Ann. "I left it entirely to my milliner, one Fanshaw, who has a great deal of taste. I never trouble myself about what I shall wear, I just give my orders and pay down the money, when they are done to my liking."

Beulah's eyes flashed, and her heightened color betrayed momentary feeling, instantly repressed.

"Mr. Markham," said she, "have you seen Mrs. Whately; I have missed her for some time."

"Yes, I saw her in the other parlour; will you take my arm, and we will find her."

Beulah gladly accepted the offer, and soon found Mrs. Whately.

"Where did you pick up that piece of vulgarity for a Rowena?" inquired Markham of his mother; "she has been grievously annoying that sweet young girl, Beulah Morris.

But that sweet girl, as you call her, must be a match for her in awkwardness. She is green from an out-of-the-world village," said Mrs Markham.

"She is perfectly lady-like in sentiment and

manners. I met her when she first started for Boston, and was with her all the way, and yet I could not summon resolution to address her without an introduction, this evening," remarked the son.

"Miss Gunn has quite a pretty fortune, I am told, and I wish you to be polite to her, and there are a great many other girls that you ought to notice before that Beulah Morris," said his mother.

But, notwithstanding the suggestion, Harriet Ann was destined to enact wall-flower the remainder of the evening, nobody taking the least notice of her.

She had given express orders to the waiter, that he should announce aloud when her carriage arrived. Accordingly, "Miss Gunn's carriage" sounded through the apartments, and every eye was directed towards her. She arose, and, instead of going to Mrs. Markham to take leave, she walked nearly to the door of the parlour, then, turning round, said in a loud voice, "Good evening, gentlemen and ladies," and then followed that courtesy, that astonishing courtesy, and Miss Gunn disappeared, — every one acknowledging that to have been the most amusing performance of the evening.

CHAPTER XVIII.

A FATHER'S LETTER.

Two weeks after the *tableaux*, Beulah received a letter from her father. We will not vouch for the authenticity of the orthography, but, in other respects, the following is a true copy.

"Dear Beulah: —

"Yours of the 18th duly received. We are all comfortable. Your mother and I have missed you unaccountably, but we are much less lonesome now Azariah has got married and fetched his wife home; a nice, industrious young woman your new sister is, just fit for a farmer's wife; — none of your hoity-toity high-flyers.

"What queer things the *live* pictures that you describe must be. I am glad our little Beulah did not show herself off to the city folks in one of them. It is never worth while to play a game with folks who know how to play it a great deal better than we do. Medad was mightily tickled to think Harriet Ann came off no better. He says, he believes now that the proud girl is so puffed up with pride, because she has got a little money, that was the reason she did not wish to know him.

"Our Medad has of late taken a great fancy for learning. He goes to school this winter, and reads and studies every night till ten or eleven.

"Now, Beulah, I must give you a little good advice. Do n't, because you are learning to play on the piano, and other fine accomplishments, do n't go for to forget that you will have one of these days to be a useful woman, and be a comfort to me and to your mother. We go for comfort, and do n't feel as if we could bear to have you come back to us spoiled, and lose all those pretty, winning ways that you used to have.

"You always was a good girl, Beulah, and if you should go far away for to change into one of them silly things, such as Medad describes, with the diddle-cum-twiddle walk, (the fellow really has some humor,) it would almost break our hearts.

"People who live in great brick houses often have very little souls,—just as you have seen a very small pea in a very large pod. And because a great many people live together where the streets and houses are so blocked up that it 's a wonder that each gets his due allowance of air to breathe,—because these people are thus jammed together in a city, it 's no reason they should think so much more of themselves, and despise country-people who have always breathed the free air of heaven, without so much as saying, 'By your leave,' to any human being.

"But, Beulah, your mother and I begin to grow somewhat oldish. We 've been a hard-working couple, and after tugging and toiling so many years we 've got together some thousands for our children. And as you won't have to begin where we did, it 's very well that you should have a better education than we did. Knowledge is a good thing if used rightly. And as to behaviour you can't have a better example than cousin Whately. Our grandmother always said, that Laura was more likely to make a perfect lady than any grandchild she had.

"But your mother and I, as I was saying, have got somewhat on the downhill of life, and we can't always jog on together. We 've got to part, and, whichever goes first, the one that 's left will need kindness from the children. Their loving hearts I hope will be the stay of our old age.

"Ever since I left off the bitters and toddy, I 've been a more sober-minded man. I thank you, dear child, for persuading me to it, and I read my Bible more, and latterly think more about dying, and being fit to die, by living well; and when you come home, Beulah, I shall want you to sit in the chimney-corner, and read the good book loud to us, and sing us sacred hymns with the sweet voice that was given you to praise your Maker.

"Give our respects to cousin Whately. I 'm glad she has proven such a good friend; — but you did right not to accept presents.

"Azariah and his wife send lots of love, in which Medad desires to join. Your mother's heart is always full to the brim of love for you, and so is that of your father,

"JOAB MORRIS.

"P. S. I am sorry to hear of the mishaps that have befallen poor Mrs. Fanshaw. Riches have wings. Tell Zephina I should be right glad to see her at our house; I hope she has n't lost her appetite. It 's very great nobleness in her to support and be so kind to her mother, — poor, wordly woman that she was. Medad's watch proves an uncommon good one, and your mother and I were pleased that he made the purchase. He is a shrewd one, or he would have got taken in. There now, I promised to leave a place for him to write a postcript, and I 've most filled up the paper."

MEDAD'S P. S. "Do n't tell any body for the world what I am going to tell you. The other day I was reading in a book of poetry and flowers, and there was a little bluish flower with four leaves, called a forget-me-not. Then I examined my watch-case, and lo and behold, it was a forget-me-not! What do you think of that, Beulah? Ask — you know who — if she knew the name of it when she worked it for me, and tell her, if she did, I will obey the command till death."

Beulah wiped away the tears that flowed abundantly during the perusal of this letter, and resolved to go immediately to see Mrs. Fanshaw

CHAPTER XIX.

AN INVALID.

Mrs. Whately took Beulah to No. 19 —— Street, and left her at a plain but respectable looking house. Beulah knocked gently at the door of a front room in the second story, and a feeble voice bade her come in. She entered.

Mrs. Fanshaw was supported by pillows in bed, so that she was nearly in a sitting posture. She looked at Beulah without recognizing her, and said, in a gentle voice, "Come nearer, if you please, Miss, that I may see who it is."

Beulah, coming near and extending her hand, replied, "It is Beulah Morris, your daughter's friend."

"Indeed!" exclaimed the invalid. "How tall you have grown!" and she was going to add, "and how very pretty," but changed it to the simple request, "Will you take a seat? I am very glad to see you."

The room was in perfect order. The counterpane on the bed was as white as snow, and the little table that stood by the bedside was covered with a clean napkin, under which were medicines, grapes, and oranges. Every thing, in short, showed the most delicate attention to the comfort of the invalid. By her side lay a Bible and one or two devotional books, which she seemed to have been reading.

Mrs. Fanshaw was extremely pale. Instead of the contemptuous, dissatisfied expression that had formerly disfigured her countenance, there was a look of quiet resignation that went directly to Beulah's heart. She expressed regret at finding her so ill.

"Thank you," replied Mrs. Fanshaw; "I ought to be grateful for relief from extreme suffering. I am sorry Zephina is not here to see you. But she has no time to spare from her daily occupation and from her poor, feeble mother. We employ a woman to prepare our meals and take care of our (*apartments*, she was going to say, but immediately corrected herself, and said, with an effort) one room."

"I saw Zephina a short time since, and she appeared quite cheerful," said Beulah.

"My noble girl is the greatest possible blessing to me," continued Mrs. Fanshaw. "You remember, Beulah, — for I must call you by the name that Zephina so dearly loves, — you remember, that I wished Zephina to become an accomplished lady. Poor, misguided woman that I was. I thought, then, only of external accomplishments. Sickness and sorrow have been the appointed messengers of good to me, and the world has so far receded that I can see it in its true light. Zephina always loved the true and the useful, and understood the real value of accomplishments better than I did. When I see her performing her arduous duties so faithfully and so cheerfully, I am ready to exclaim,

> 'There is a beauty in her daily life
> That makes my own look ugly.'"

There was a momentary pause, and then Beulah mentioned her father's letter, and his kind remembrance of Zephina, and his desire to have her make a visit at Baxter.

"What generous kindness!" exclaimed the invalid; "and do you know, Beulah, that, in my foolish and wicked heart, I despised country people, and called them vulgar?"

"You did not become acquainted with them, and therefore could not judge with regard to their character or manners," kindly replied Beulah.

"How seldom do we meet with such disinterested kindness as you have shown to Zephina!" continued Mrs. Fanshaw. "Harriet Ann Gunn has become quite rich, and now she never comes to see us. She passes Zephina in the street, and cuts her deliberately."

"If it would afford you any pleasure," said Beulah, "I should like to come and read to you quite often. Zephina says it fatigues you to read."

"I should be exceedingly obliged to you, for of late my eyes are weak; I am so much alone that I have relied upon these for my companions," said the invalid, laying her hand upon the Bible and her other books.

Beulah then rose to go, — leaving her best love for Zephina, and a little note, which she laid upon the table. It was Medad's postscript, in an envelope, with a few lines from Beulah herself.

CHAPTER XX.

HARRIET ANN AT HOME.

Mr. Prium was, as Mrs. Markham had said a very respectable man, and his wife an excellent woman.

Mr. Gunn died insolvent, soon after Harriet Ann returned from Baxter, and left her penniless. Mrs. Prium, his sister, received his orphan into her family, and her husband freely gave her a home. She had been with this kind family about a year when a brother much older than herself, who had been absent many years, died, and left her a pretty fortune, — she thought it immense.

Feeling the added consequence that this unexpected good fortune gave her, she began to despise her kind benefactors. She went to school, and there made herself ridiculous by her pretension. Whenever any new acquaintances walked towards home with her, she would go half a mile out of the way rather than to have them see her enter her uncle's house.

One day, as she was coming from school with two of her schoolmates, a sudden shower came up, and one of the girls proposed that they should take an omnibus.

"An omnibus!" exclaimed Harriet Ann. "I am horrified! I should be ashamed to be seen in an omnibus, they are so shocking vulgar. What would folks think of us!"

"I do n't care what they think," said the girl who had made the proposal. "Here comes one. Let 's jump in." And they were soon in the coach, Harriet Ann not being willing to be left alone in the rain.

The coach was somewhat crowded. "Can't you move, woman?" said Harriet Ann to a most respectable looking person.

"Perhaps I could, if you were to request it more politely," she replied.

"Who expects politeness in an omnibus!" demanded Harrriet Ann, in an exceedingly impertinent manner.

"Every lady," was the laconic reply.

When they were not far from Mr. Prium's

door, Harriet Ann said to her companions, "I have got to get out on an errand at a house just above, and there I can borrow an umbrella to go home. Boy, stop at Mr. Prium's."

"Mr. Prium, the baker?" said the boy.

"Yes; I believe he is a baker, or some such sort of a thing," she muttered.

The coach stopped, and out came Mr. Prium with an umbrella. "Harriet Ann," said the good man, as he stepped to the coach to help her out, "I was just going for thee, I am glad thee has got home without a wetting."

"Is n't that too bad!" exclaimed one of her companions. "That was her uncle. How kindly he spoke to her, and what a fine-looking man he is. How can she despise him!"

"He is one of the most benevolent men in the world, and universally respected," said the lady to whom Harriet Ann had so rudely spoken; "and that I suppose is the orphan whom he received into his house out of charity. Mistaken girl! She may disgrace her uncle, but his relationship would be an honor to any one."

Thus the foolish stratagem and the wicked falsehood were perfectly understood, and met with the contempt that they merited.

Mr. Prium's mother lived in his family, a venerable woman of eighty, to whom the whole household, with one exception, paid the most deferential respect. "Come, get up, granny, you are on my work," said Harriet Ann, who had taken the large chair especially appropriated to the aged grandmother, and had left her own work in it when the good old lady happened to be out of the room. "Come, get up quick, I wish you would not always be poking yourself in every body's way."

"My eyesight is failing, child, and I did not see your work," replied she, mildly.

"Well, people that are so old are always in the way. They might at least stay in their own room," said the rude girl.

Those aged eyes, from which no tears had fallen for many a year, now filled, and the large drops rolled over the withered cheeks. "Merciful God! I thank thee, that thou hast given thy servant good and dutiful children," fervently ejaculated the venerable woman.

Mr. Prium had just entered the door and heard this conversation. "Harriet Ann Gunn," said he, "how durst thee speak thus to my respected mother! Thee calls thyself a lady; is this the proof? Gray hairs are a crown of glory when found, like my blessed mother's, in the way of righteousness. Contempt for the aged is a meanness as well as a sin."

"I forgive her, and so must thee, Thomas; in giddy girlhood there is much thoughtlessness," said the saintlike woman.

"Yet youth, my good mother, is the season for gentleness and affection," replied Mr. Prium, "and she who lacks these amiable qualities in the spring-time of life, will be cold hearted before its summer, and frozen into very ice long before its autumn."

"That is quite a poetical speech for a Quaker," said the incorrigible girl, upon whom it seemed impossible to make one favorable impression.

"Thy heart is already ice, Harriet Ann," he replied, with more severity than he was ever known to use in his whole life before; "and the mistaken man, who should take thee to his bosom for a wife, would find thee a viper there."

CHAPTER XXI.

AN AWKWARD ACQUAINTANCE.

As Mrs. Whately and her young friend were going to church one Sunday, the latter suddenly exclaimed, "There comes Dr. Weasenby! Shall I try the Boston fashion of cutting an acquaintance?"

"By no means, Beulah; I am sure you would not do such a foolish thing," replied Mrs Whately.

"Not unless you wish it, I certainly should not," was the reply.

Sure enough, there was "the doctor's young man," more starched and stiff-necked than ever, dressed in a complete suit of glossy black. He bowed in the most formal manner, and then came to a full stand, extending his hand to Beulah in a new yellow glove, so unpliable that he could not bend his fingers.

There was the slightest possible degree of condescension in Beulah's manner as she touched the tips of those awkward fingers, and politely returned the bow. Dr. Weasenby saw nothing but the greatest cordiality in her manner, and inquired where she was going to church.

"I am going with Mrs. Whately to church."

The Doctor, taking this for an introduction to the lady, raised his hat straight up a quarter of a yard above his head without inclining it an inch, and then settled it so carefully as not to disturb a single hair. "Well, I will wait upon you, ladies," said he, just as Mrs. Whately was going to invite him.

"How long is it since you were in Baxter, Sir?" asked Beulah.

"Three weeks, precisely. I asked the Squire to write to you, but just then it was a special busy time, and he could n't. He 's nicely, and so is the old woman," replied the Doctor.

'And my brothers, they are well, I suppose, or I should have heard of it," said Beulah.

"They are both smart. Baxter is an amazing healthy place, and I have come to settle in Boston, where it 's more sickly."

No sooner were they seated in church, than

Dr. Weasenby smoothed up his hair in front, and down behind, in his own peculiar manner. A loud whispering and half-suppressed tittering was heard in the pew behind them. It was Harriet Ann and her constant companion, Miss Stiltaker. They were vastly amused with the specimen of a country beau before them, and kept their heads together, whispering under each other's bonnets, during the whole time they were in church, to the great annoyance of those who were near them.

Dr. Weasenby, on the contrary, was reverential in his manner, and Mrs. Whately was not in the least troubled because the stranger with her happened not to be quite as elegant in his appearance as her acquaintances generally were.

As soon as service was over, and Beulah had stepped out of the pew, she was seized rudely by Harriet Ann, who whispered in her ear, loud enough to startle those in their neighbourhood, "Why, Beulah Morris, who have you got with you? That poke-a-moonshine, I mean." Beulah was quite too much surprised to answer immediately, and the rude girl continued, "He is indubitably a Baxter man, I know him by the cut of his hair."

Beulah whispered, very low, "I am afraid he will hear you. He is a young physician, who has just established himself in Boston."

"Is it possible!" exclaimed Harriet Ann, whose opinion seemed to undergo a very sudden change. "I had n't an idea that he was a professional man."

By this time they were at the door, and, their way homeward being in different directions, they parted. Dr. Weasenby accompanied Mrs. Whately and Beulah, and when they reached home, Mrs. Whately very politely asked him to walk in.

"Not now," said the Doctor, "but I shall try to call very soon."

"That is rather an awkward young man," remarked Mrs. Whately, when they had entered the house, "but by no means so vulgar as those silly girls who sat giggling at him in church. I have often noticed them at concerts and lectures. Instead of listening themselves, they prevent others from hearing by their continual whispering; and now and then comes a derisive laugh from them, which proves they are amusing themselves by ridiculing every one. In the street, too, their rude impertinence is almost insulting. I have repeatedly heard the inquiry made, 'Who is that very vulgar girl with the long light curls?' Beulah, dear, you must be civil to her, but she is so encroaching and obtrusive, that it is necessary to treat her with great coolness."

There was nothing in the circumstances or appearance of Harriet Ann Gunn that prevented her from becoming a lady. Every one must acknowledge that it was entirely her own fault that she could not be received into the society which she sought with bold pertinacity.

CHAPTER XXII.

A FRIEND IN AFFLICTION.

THE next time that Beulah visited Mrs. Fanshaw, she purchased on the way a beautiful bouquet to place upon her little table.

The invalid received the attention gratefully. "I love flowers, now," said she, "better than I ever did before in my life; they are indeed the 'poetry of earth,' as the stars are 'the poetry of heaven.' Every thing that speaks to me of the wisdom and goodness of the Creator now gives me unspeakable pleasure. My young friend, do you know how indifferent I was to all these things when I was in the country?"

"I know you went out very little," replied Beulah.

"Uncover those ottomans, if you please," said she, pointing to two large seats covered with brown linen. "There was my bane. I labored over those, and several other pieces of embroidery, until I ruined my health. I loved all artificial things better than the true and natural, — artificial manners, artificial enjoyments, and even artificial flowers, better than natural ones. I could not but apply to myself some lines that I read the other day, from one of the English poets. Here they are; will you read this stanza for me?"

Beulah read the following lines, from Beattie's "Minstrel":

"O, how canst thou renounce the boundless store
Of charms which Nature to her votary yields?
The warbling woodland, the resounding shore,
The pomp of groves, the garniture of fields;
All that the genial ray of morning gilds,
And all that echoes to the song of even,
All that the mountain's sheltering bosom shields,
And all the dread magnificence of Heaven;
O, how canst thou renounce, and hope to be forgiven?"

"How much I might have enjoyed had I loved the country as Zephina did. Her sweetest recollections are of those beautiful scenes about your native village," remarked Mrs. Fanshaw.

"Could you not go into the country for a while," said Beulah; "it would be beneficial to both of you."

"No, my dear young lady, I never shall behold again in life groves and green fields," solemnly replied the invalid.

"But my father and mother, I am sure, would do every thing in their power to make it pleasant to you, if you and Zephina would pay them a visit," replied Beulah, not understanding the allusion.

"Your kindness makes me ashamed of myself. Too well do I remember the pride and wickedness of my heart, the only time that I ever entered their hospitable dwelling. There was a lady from a distance then visiting you. Do you remember who it was, and where she lives?"

"Her name was Mrs. Whately, and she lives in Boston," replied Beulah.

"Ah, I see it all; you are with her now. Zephina did not tell me, I suspect, for fear it would revive painful remembrances. And your cousin knows of your coming to my humble room, and does not disapprove of it?"

"She would be most happy to come herself, and testify the interest she feels for you and for Zephina," replied Beulah.

"She is very kind; she can do nothing for me, but she may do much to befriend my desolate child when I am gone." The invalid's voice faltered, and she changed the subject.

"You kindly promised to read to me, Beulah, and will you do me the favor to turn to the parable of the Prodigal Son? There is no part of the Bible so touching, and at the same time so consoling, as the teachings of our blessed Saviour."

Beulah found the parable, and read it in that sweet, soothing tone, so grateful to an ear rendered sensitive by long illness, and a heart bowed down with many sorrows.

When the reading was ended, Mrs. Fanshaw said, "Thus have I wandered from my Father's house, and, as the shadows of life's close gather around me, I look back upon the enjoyments that I once sought with such avidity as indeed dry husks. Would that I had sooner learned the true value of this probationary existence."

Beulah now took leave, promising to call again very soon. "My dear Beulah, *you* have early learned the pleasure of doing good; God bless you," was the invalid's parting benediction.

Only a few days after this visit, a messenger was sent in great haste for Beulah, saying that Mrs. Fanshaw was dangerously ill. Beulah was just dressing for a concert, to which she was going with Mrs. Whately. Immediately she resumed her plain dress, and, the carriage being at the door, went instantly to her afflicted friend.

Mrs. Fanshaw had been seized with paralysis, and the physician who had been summoned pronounced the case a hopeless one. Her face was terribly distorted, so that it was fearful to look upon. Zephina was bathing her forehead, and attempting every possible means of relief. Beulah resolved to remain with her, and despatched the coachman to beg permission of Mrs. Whately. She readily granted it, and sent her own woman to assist in any way that might be needful.

After a few hours, the distorted features relaxed, a calm expression stole over them, and all suffering seemed to have passed away. And, in that silent chamber,

"They watched her breathing through the night,
Her breathing soft and low,
As in her breast the wave of life
Kept heaving to and fro.

"And when the morn rose dim and sad,
And chill with early showers,
Her quiet eyelids closed; — she had
Another morn than theirs."

CHAPTER XXIII.

ZEPHINA'S GRIEF.

And there sat Zephina alone watching the dead. Beulah had taken her home with her, for a few hours, on that sad morning. When she returned, the room was in the neatest possible order, and the corpse, in the habiliments of the grave, lay upon the bedstead. No entreaties on the part of Mrs. Whately could induce the devoted girl to leave the lifeless form of her mother. There she remained in the chamber of death, in the absorbed quietness of deep grief. She had been the heart's idol of that mother, and, whatever had been the errors or the foibles of the departed, they were all forgotten. Zephina remembered only her love and kindness. And what earthly love is so pure, or so disinterested? Who, that has known the deep tenderness of a mother's love, is not ready to answer, from a full heart, "Such was the love of my own dear mother."

Without any care on the part of Zephina, every thing was arranged for the funeral on the following day. Even all her mourning clothes were sent to her in perfect order. Her only remaining relations were distant ones, who lived in a remote part of the country.

When the hour for the funeral arrived, Mrs. Whately and Beulah came with the clergyman, and four of Mrs. Whately's friends as pall-bearers. The solemn services were performed. Mrs. Whately's carriage contained all the mourners, for that kind lady and Beulah sympathized so truly with the desolate Zephina, that the mourning garb they wore was neither a mere form, nor a solemn mockery. As they wound through one of those beautiful paths at Mount Auburn, so calm was Zephina that one not acquainted with grief would have said that she did not feel deeply, — but what agony is like that which finds no outward expression? The only dry eyes at that grave were those of the chief mourner, when the earth fell upon that coffin, and she was a friendless orphan. No, not friendless; for when the carriage stopped, it was at Mrs. Whately's door and when Zephina hesitated a moment, at Beulah's tone of gentle entreaty, "Dear Zephina," she allowed herself to be conducted into the house.

Zephina passed a week with Mrs. Whately, and then, although urged to remain longer, she went back to her lonely and desolate room, and to her daily employment. Her character was so truly noble, that it could not fail to make a strong impression.

"How lovely Zephina looks in her deep mourning suit," said Mrs. Whately. "She never seemed so sweet and amiable before. It would be difficult to find any one more lady-like. From a refined delicacy of feeling towards her departed mother, she now takes special care to cultivate all the exterior marks of a well-bred woman. I admire, too, her self-respect. No employment, — even though considered far below the respectable one in which she is engaged, — no honorable employment could degrade such an elevated and truly dignified character."

Such praise bestowed upon her friend, and coming, too, from those ever-truthful lips, made Beulah's warm heart throb, and tears come gushing into her eyes; — for, ever, when

"She heard the praise of those she loved,
The mantling blood, in ready play,
Rivalled the blush of early day."

Zephina's employment kept her so constantly engaged, that for a time she saw very little of Beulah. This sadly grieved them both. Mrs. Whately, although she did not receive company on Sunday, invited Zephina to pass that day with them, and they would not consider her a visiter. It should be her Sabbath home. And so indeed it became, for Zephina would not resist such kindness. All through the week, she pursued, contentedly, her employment, inspiring every one who met her with respect, living entirely alone, yet cheered with the pleasant anticipation of the blessed day of rest, the soothing sympathy and kindness of Beulah, and the wise counsel of Mrs. Whately.

CHAPTER XXIV.

HOME.

Beulah's visit, at the earnest entreaty of her friend, had been prolonged from time to time until the Squire's patience was quite exhausted, and Mrs. Morris said she could not spare her another month. Mrs. Whately was compelled to yield to their urgency, and, hearing of a lady who was going directly through Baxter, she placed Beulah under her care, and she arrived in due time, without accident, at home.

And was Beulah unfitted for home by her long absence, and a different mode of living? No; she entered with new interest into all the affairs of the family. She aided her mother in household concerns, and soon, without adding materially to their expenses, gave an air of taste and refinement to the interior arrangements of the farm house.

"How did you make out with your hundred a year, Beulah, among so many fine folks," inquired Squire Morris, after Beulah had been home a few weeks.

"O, very well, father, as you will see by my account-book. I was obliged to be more economical than I at first expected, but, as I did not wish to dress extravagantly, I had every thing that so young a girl needed.

"And you accepted no presents from cousin Whately?" continued he.

"Certainly not, after your request, father."

The Squire looked over the account, praised its neatness, and run over the figures to see that they had been summed up correctly.

"Keep that, my child, it 's a credit to you," said he, returning the account-book. "You will make a smart, orderly woman, just like your namesake. It 's the best praise I can bestow upon you to say, that you deserve the name of my mother; — excepting always present company," added the Squire, shutting one eye, and looking with the other at his wife. "Mary *is* a pretty good name."

One of the first visits that Beulah made after her return was to the poor blind woman.

"How do you do, Nancy?" said Beulah.

The woman started up, and, extending her hand, said, "That sweet voice can come only from little Beulah Morris. And yet it is softer and gentler than ever. They have not spoiled you."

Little did poor Nancy imagine, that the *little* Beulah was a tall, graceful girl, almost seventeen years old.

"And who has led you to church during my absence," asked Beulah.

"Your kind brother, Medad. At first I felt awkwardly to be led by such a tall boy, but I got used to it, and liked it in time, for he has a strong arm to lean on, and a strong heart, too, Beulah. Very few boys would have done such a kindness."

All the other neighbours were visited in turn, and it was pleasant to hear them say, "Why, Beulah Morris has n't grown a bit proud and ceremonious; she is just the same girl, only a great deal more warm-hearted."

Medad, whose intelligence had been increasing, and who had seen several other places besides Baxter, proposed that the farm-house should be painted white, and a porch added to the front-door. Moreover, his taste was not quite satisfied till green blinds were added, and a new fence, with a neat gateway. When these improvements were completed, and the garden and front-yard put in nice order, every body said, there was not so fine a looking house in all Baxter.

Azariah and his wife were comfortably established in a pretty cottage not far distant from the farm-house, and soon after Beulah's return they invited the young people of the neighbourhood to come and spend the afternoon, and take tea. Beulah was much pleased to find Azariah's wife a sensible, discerning woman, with much more cultivation of mind than she had expected.

Azariah very naturally inquired, " Well, wife, how do you like our Beulah ? "

" I think I shall love her very much," she replied ; " one can see at the first glance that she is amiable. Then I like her manners, better, I think, than any young girl's that I ever saw. Did you ever notice that she never interrupts any body in conversation, not even a domestic ? When she is talking with old Cato, she waits as patient as a lamb till he gets through one of his tedious speeches, and seems as much interested as if he really was talking very much to the purpose."

"It 's nothing new; she always had just those pretty ways. Have you heard her play on the piano; — they say she was asked to play everywhere in Boston," said Azariah, looking quite proudly.

"I have not, excepting some psalm-tunes last Sunday evening," replied the wife.

"Well, you could n't hear her then, for father and Medad sang Old Hundred, and Mear, and their other old tunes, so loud, that you could n't hardly have heard a bass-drum, if there had been one there," said Azariah.

"I noticed Beulah particularly the other evening when we had company," said Mrs. Azariah Morris. "She sat in a corner where there was tattling and gossiping and scandal going on, and she was perfectly quiet, but I could see she looked a little sad, as if it gave her pain. She never contradicts you, Azariah, and when you make a mistake never corrects you. I thought she would be for instructing us in a great many new ways, but she seems to think we are doing very well, and never makes any comparisons about our house or furniture, and never boasts of having seen any thing more expensive. For my part, I should be quite willing to be told any thing from her that would improve our country ways."

"O, I guess we shall jog along, wife, pretty well after the old ways;—but I 'm glad you really like our Beulah"

CHAPTER XXV.

AN INTENDED MARRIAGE.

ZEPHINA had in one of her letters mentioned that she was not very well. One evening she had just returned home, lighted her lamp, and seated herself in her lonely room, when she was startled by a loud rap at the door. Alarmed, she opened it with a trembling hand, and there stood Squire Morris.

"Finey, my dear child, is it you?" said he; "you are so altered I hardly knew you."

"My kind Squire Morris!" exclaimed she; "you have n't altered in the least. Come in, Sir; will you?"

The Squire took a seat, and looked around the room, — then he seemed troubled with a sudden cold, — or at least he wiped his eyes as he said, 'Finey, you live here all alone. That is n't right. I 've come for you to take you to Baxter, for my Beulah has pined for you ever since she got home."

"You have come all this distance to take me to Baxter!" exclaimed Zephina. "What kindness!"

"O, no very great kindness on my part," said the Squire; "the kindness will all be on your side if you will consent to go. Can you be ready by day after to-morrow?"

Zephina was silent for some moments.

"O, I forgot," said the kind-hearted man; — "here is a little billet from Beulah that will persuade you better than I can."

Zephina's tears fell fast upon the paper as she read the note, — but they were tears of joy. "I did not need this to persuade me," said she, folding it up, and kissing it. "It is enough that you have taken all this trouble for me. I will go."

"Thank you, thank you," said the Squire. "And can I help you any way about getting ready?"

"O, no; what little arrangements I have to make will soon be completed." And Zephina looked sorrowfully around her room, as she said, "I shall leave every thing here as it is, till my return."

"Well, then, good night; I stop with Cousin Whately, and shall not see you again till day after to-morrow morning, bright and early. You look pale, dear. *Miss* Morris says country air always suited you, and she knows now it will be the best medicine in the world for you."

"There is no medicine like kindness for the sick heart," said Zephina.

All needful arrangements were made on the following day, and Zephina was ready at the appointed hour. Yet it was sad to leave that place, enchained as it was to so many touching remembrances. Amid much sorrow and loneliness, she had passed there many hours of peace and contentment.

And Baxter was at last in sight, first the steeple, then the village.

"But where is the dear farm-house?" eagerly inquired Zephina.

"Here we are home again," said the Squire, as they stopped before the gate.

"What, this white house with green blinds?" exclaimed Zephina, with a momentary feeling of disappointment that it was not the same old red house. And then she added, "It is! it is! for there comes Beulah through that pretty porch." And another was there who was not named, and a more cordial welcome could not have been given to the heiress of millions.

And after the greetings were over, there were many improvements to be shown to Zephina. The bower had been enlarged, or rather built anew with more durable materials, and it was completely covered with sweet-briers and honey-suckles.

And there, not many weeks after, a conversation took place, which decided the future life of Zephina, — a conversation in which Medad was the other party, and the principal speaker.

The Squire insisted, that there was no use in putting off what was to be done, and what every body allowed was the best thing that could have happened. He wanted the young folks to be married right away; for he took all the credit to himself of having brought it about, — though he did allow that Medad hinted pretty hard about his going after Zephina.

"But," said the good man confidentially to Mrs. Morris, "when I saw how handsome Finey had grown, and how sort of stately and graceful she was, like a tall, young elm-tree, my heart went pit-a-pat for the boy, just as it did when I popped the question to you, wife ; and I think he is a lucky fellow to get such a prize ; but he is a first-rate farmer, and he deserves her, — though he is our son."

Zephina consented to name an early day, and in bright and beautiful June, when the rose-season offered its sweetest gifts, they were married.

Soon after the marriage, they went to Boston, not for the sake of a fashionable bridal-tour, but because the bride had made no arrangements, when she left the city, with reference to the event that had taken place.

The very day that they arrived in Boston, by one of those singular coincidences that do now and then happen, Harriet Ann Gunn's name was ringing louder than it ever had done before. She did not appear at breakfast one morning. Caleb Prium required that every one should be punctual in his family, and sent a servant-girl to call her. The girl came down, saying that she had knocked at her door, and called, but that no one had answered, and she *believed* the door was fastened.

Mrs. Prium went and found that it was so, and, alarmed lest her niece should be ill or dead, called her husband, and he immediately burst the door open, — but no Harriet Ann was there

The bureau drawers were opened, and every thing of value taken out of them, — her trunks and bandboxes all gone. They at first thought of a robbery, — but then what had become of Harriet Ann herself? So great was their alarm, that the girl who had been sent to call her at length confessed that she had helped her to pack her trunks, and to remove all her luggage in the night to the front door, and that very early in the morning a carriage had come, and, as she expressed it, "Had taken the bandboxes, and baskets, and trunks, and Miss Harriet Ann, all away."

"And who came in the carriage?"

She did not know; — she did n't go to the door.

Just then the opposite neighbour, who kept a grocery store, came over, and asked if Caleb Prium knew who his niece had gone away with?

No; certainly he did not.

Well, then, he could tell him; for he was opening his shop very early, and he saw a carriage drive very slowly up to the door, and, said he, "Out jumped that rascal who calls himself Mr. Percy, from South Carolina."

"And who is he?" demanded Mr. Prium.

"As great a scamp as ever lived. He owes me ten or twelve dollars for cigars and wine. I just discovered yesterday that his true name is Mark Timberley, and that he has been in the Philadelphia Penitentiary. But do n't let us stop to say any more about him, for I heard him tell the driver to take them to the Providence Railroad, and the cars have n't gone out yet. You may find them before they get off."

Mr. Prium waited for nothing but to put on his broad-brimmed beaver, and reached the *depôt* just as the cars were starting. He jumped on, however, and went to Providence. There, the first persons whom he saw come from the cars were Mr. Percy and Miss Gunn.

Caleb Prium immediately stepped up to them, and, addressing Mr. Percy in a low tone, said, "Thee need n't trouble thyself to conduct my niece any farther, Mark Timberley. I will do that myself. Harriet Ann, take my arm, if thee does not wish to be led to the Philadelphia Penitentiary."

Harriet Ann dropped the arm upon which she had been leaning, and Mr. Percy, *alias* Mark Timberley, walked off, very, very fast, indeed. Caleb Prium attended to the luggage, and, taking the next train back to Boston, without a word of explanation, conducted Harriet Ann quietly back to his own house. He handed her out of the carriage, led her into the front parlour, and closed the door.

"Harriet Ann, where was thee going?" said he.

"Going to be married to Mr. Percy," was the reply.

"He was a villain. Where is thee going now?" continued Caleb Prium.

"Going!" exclaimed the astonished girl; "where should I go?"

"The carriage waits for thee to decide. I cannot have thee stay under my roof till thee learns to respect thyself," said the Quaker decidedly.

"Forgive me, O, forgive me, for mercy's sake, Uncle Prium, and I will listen to your advice and try to be all that you wish," said Harriet Ann, with streaming eyes and clasped hands.

"And can thee give up thy foolish, mistaken notions of being a lady, and try to become a good and useful woman?" asked he.

"I will, I will indeed, for I know I am nothing now but a silly girl, who has been led away by wrong notions."

"There, now, thee is coming to thy senses. God grant that thy penitential tears may have their well-spring in thy heart." And Caleb Prium ordered the coachman to bring in the luggage.

Mrs. Prium's curiosity led her to make further inquiries of Harriet Ann. She learned that Percy, *alias* Timberley, had attracted her attention first in the street, by a pair of large, dark eyes, black, curling hair, whiskers and mustaches, and by his splendid and fashionable dress; that he had found an opportunity to be introduced to her, and had often met her at her friend, Miss Stiltaker's. He pretended to be a rich Southern planter, and had induced Harriet Ann to elope with him on the plea that he knew positively that her uncle would never consent to her marriage with a Southerner, — a plea utterly false, for Caleb Prium was not a narrow-minded, prejudiced man.

Harriet Ann's head was filled with silly, romantic notions, and she thought it would be a very brilliant affair to elope with Mr. Percy, — one that would make a great noise in the fashionable world, and be announced in the newspapers through the length and breadth of the land.

In the cars he had taken her purse and watch *for safe keeping*, and that may account, in part, for his going off upon a full trot when Caleb Prium met him at Providence.

CHAPTER XXVI.

A NEW FRIEND.

It was a glorious sunset, after a lovely day in June. The evening star was just showing its silvery light in the soft, blue western sky. The Morris family were seated in the porch. Thoughts sweet and pensive, thoughts of early childhood, were gliding through the mind of Beulah Morris. They were interrupted by the stopping of a carriage at the gate.

"It is Mrs. Whately's carriage," exclaimed she, almost flying down the front-yard.

The coach-door was opened, and out stepped a tall, fine-looking young man, who handed out Mrs. Whately. Beulah was in her arms in a moment, and, after the cordial embrace, Mrs. Whately turned to her companion and introduced him as her son, Winthrop Whately.

By this time the Squire had joined them. "Welcome, welcome to Baxter, Cousin Whately," was his hearty salutation. "Happy to see you, and your son too, for I suppose this is Winthrop. Why, I have n't seen you since you were six years old, and yet I should have known you the world over; you 've got the real Morris nose. Come in, come in. Coachman," he continued, "drive into that big gate yonder, and put your horses in that new barn; this time, Cousin Whately, I shan't allow you to send them to the tavern."

And kind Mrs. Morris came forward with her welcome, and there was wondering how Mrs. Whately could have spared her only son five years, and warm congratulations upon his return, — and then it was proposed that they should enjoy the balmy evening in the porch.

"But supper, supper," said the Squire.

"But that will do two or three hours hence," Mrs. Whately said, taking a seat in the porch.

'How tastefully you have arranged your garden and grounds, and fitted up the house. And, Beulah, you love roses as well as ever, I see, by that sweet bud in your hair."

Beulah's blush at this allusion rivalled the damask bud that she had carelessly placed in her dark hair.

"Yes," replied the Squire; "young folks will have their notions; Medad and Beulah have made all these improvements."

"The rose-bushes have grown almost as much as yourself, Beulah, since I was here five years since. By the way, where is Zephina? You wrote me that she was still paying you a visit, a short time since."

"Married and gone to Boston," replied Squire Morris.

"Married!" exclaimed Mrs. Whately; "and to whom?"

"To our Medad, to be sure; the boy had set his heart upon her ever since he was seventeen years old. We managed it nicely," said the Squire, rubbing his hands with delight, "and he has gone to Boston with the prettiest bride in all New England. They will settle down here in Baxter, — good comfortable farmers, — for though I 've allowed them to slick up the old place, I go for comfort as much as ever."

Mrs. Whately expressed great pleasure at this event, saying that she regretted not being able to see the happy couple in either place, and praising Zephina so warmly as to satisfy even the Squire's partial fondness for his daughter-in-law.

The bountiful supper was soon upon the table, and presented no such glaring incongruities as formerly.

Winthrop Whately had left home much out of health, five years before, and travelled in Europe for two years with an excellent tutor. Having thus regained his health, he remained three years at the University of Gottingen, and had returned home about a month previous to this visit.

It would be difficult to describe Winthrop Whately, for his face was one of those intellectual and expressive ones, in which you seem not to discern clearly a single feature. You see it as a whole, full of life and soul, demonstrating the character; yet no one would have called it a very handsome face. His person, too, was fine, but it was a noble carriage and graceful movements that gave it its manly beauty. Mrs. Whately looked at him with a mother's affection, and perhaps a little of a mother's pride, for he had been left from his infancy entirely to her care and management, and had ever yielded to her control with affectionate docility.

Very early the next morning, Beulah was going with a pitcher of soup to Nancy, the poor blind woman. She had not proceeded far from home, when Rover came running after her, delighted to see her, and jumped with his great paws upon her shoulder, causing the soup to be spilled. "Go away, Rover, you trouble me," said she, in a beseeching tone, but the playful dog continued to jump and gambol around her, the soup all the while pouring over the top of the pitcher and down its sides, and upon her apron.

While in this awkward predicament, who should appear but Winthrop Whately, coming towards her. Beulah wore a large sun-bonnet, which concealed her face, and her simple morning-dress was so entirely different from the one she had worn the evening before, that Winthrop did not recognize her. He drove away the dog, saying, "If you will go on, Miss, I will wait and see that he does not trouble you again."

"Thank you, Mr. Whately," replied Beulah. "Rover is quite lonely in the absence of his master, and glad to see a friend. He does not know how much mischief he has done."

"Miss Morris! is it possible!" exclaimed Winthrop. "I did not expect to meet you so early in the morning; allow me to relieve you from the pitcher, which you appear to have had much trouble in carrying."

"If you please," said she, "at least till I have taken off my soiled apron. I surely did not think of your being an early riser."

"I love the morning," continued he, holding the pitcher, while Beulah took off the soiled apron, and, folding it, wrapped it around the dripping vessel. "Early rising," added he, "is not so much a duty with me as a pleasure; I owe my restoration to health in part to this habit, and being once fixed, it is a very easy one to continue."

"There, now, I can do very well; I am obliged to you," said Beulah, offering to retake the pitcher. "Poor Nancy will have but a small breakfast this morning."

"No; please let me carry it for you, and tell me who it is for whose breakfast you are so anxious."

"A poor blind woman, who lives quite alone not far distant. The neighbours take care of her, and I should have sent the soup this morning, but, hearing last evening that she was ill, I thought I would take it to her myself, and make some inquiries about the poor, lonely creature."

They were soon at the door of a small, brown house, where Beulah knocked, but no one bade her enter. She knocked again, and a feeble voice said, "Come in."

"I fear Nancy is very ill," said Beulah, as she took the pitcher from Winthrop; "if I should not be home in time to join the family at breakfast, have the kindness to make my apology."

"Allow me to wait without a while," said he "should she be quite ill, she may need other assistance than yours, and I can go for some kind neighbour."

"Thank you, I will see how she is," and Beulah entered. The poor woman lay almost lifeless and deathly pale.

"My good Nancy, are you very ill?" tenderly asked Beulah.

"Is it you, Beulah?" faintly articulated the woman.

"Yes; I have brought you some soup, can you take a little?"

"No; water, fresh, cool water," was the reply.

Beulah went to the door and handed a cup to Winthrop, requesting him to draw deep from the old well a cup of cold water. He did so; while Beulah threw aside her sun-bonnet, arranged neatly the covering of the bed, and opened the windows to admit the fresh air of the morning. When she attempted to give the water to Nancy, she found that the poor creature could not swallow without being raised up, and it was impossible for her to do it, and at the same time give her the water. Nancy's eagerness for it was intense. "Water, cold water," she repeated.

Beulah, without further hesitation, called in Winthrop to her assistance, for she feared the poor woman was dying. He came and raised her tenderly, while Beulah held the water to her lips. She drank it with avidity and was somewhat revived.

"Beulah, my child," said she, "I am almost gone; send for some one to be with me."

"I will, Nancy. I have a friend here who will go for any one you will name. Can you lie down now?"

"I will try; it is a strong arm and a strange one that supports me, I thank *him*, whoever it is."

And Winthrop, placing the blind woman's head gently upon her pillow, withdrew his arm, much wondering at this quickness of perception.

"Beulah, my sweet child, how kind you have always been to me. May God reward you, but I am too sick now for your youthful experience. Send for Nurse White," said Nancy. "I shall not need any one long."

Beulah now stepped to the door with Winthrop, and pointed out to him the house of Nurse White, saying she would wait until she came. Winthrop went, reflecting with surprise on the readiness with which that delicate young girl remained alone with the dying blind woman.

Beulah sat down by the bedside. Nancy was for a while silent, excepting a low, indistinct moaning, at intervals. At length she said, "I cannot collect my thoughts, and I wish to pray. Will you pray with me, Beulah?"

Beulah knelt by the bedside, clasped her hands, and, lifting her eyes to heaven, uttered a short and fervent petition in behalf of the dying woman.

As Winthrop returned to say that the nurse would soon be there, he passed by the low, open window, and the touching scene within met his eye. He saw that youthful countenance uplifted while the heart was in communion with the Father of spirits, and the scriptural expression, "the beauty of holiness," was for the first time revealed to him, in all its fulness of meaning.

Towards evening of the same day, Beulah glided out unobserved, and went to inquire after Nancy. When she reached the door, Nurse White met her, and informed her that the poor woman had died a few hours after she left in the morning.

Beulah asked why they had not sent to her father's for any assistance that might have been needed.

"O," said the nurse, "the good young gentleman that came for me this morning left his purse with me, begging me to see that poor Nancy wanted for nothing. But that is not all; he was here when she died, and no one else was with her but me, and he was so kind and gentle, and gave such sweet consolation to the dying woman, — equal to any minister. And poor Nancy had her reason to the last, and blessed the stranger with her dying breath. I told him the neighbours, would have taken care of her, and paid the expenses of her funeral, for they had always been kind to her; but he only said, if they had enjoyed the privilege of doing good so long, he ought to have the opportunity now. And he was very urgent, that I should not tell all this to any one, but I thought I might just mention it to you, because you always took such an interest in the poor soul who is now at rest."

Beulah walked thoughtfully homeward, and on her way she was joined by Winthrop, but their walk was almost a silent one; they were too much inclined to serious meditation, at that soft, twilight hour, after the solemn events of the day, to be communicative. Yet they had in that single day become better acquainted with each other's true character than they would have done in the ordinary intercourse of society, in months, or perhaps years.

CHAPTER XXVII.

THE FUTURE MOTHER-IN-LAW.

"WELL, Cousin Winthrop," said Squire Morris, three or four days after the arrival of the Whatelys, "well, Cousin Winthrop, what did you see in foreign countries equal to these United States?"

"Not any thing that I love half as well," he replied.

"Now I like that," continued the Squire; "you have n't come home, then, as some youngsters do, puffed up with pride, despising Yankees. I am right glad that you have brought back a good, sound, healthy heart, true to your own kith and kin."

"Perfectly so," replied Winthrop; "I never loved them half as well before."

"And what are you going to do for the good of your own country, now you have travelled and got knowledge at a foreign University?"

"I am thinking of being a lawyer; partly because it was the profession of my father and my grandfather, and because I think I am perhaps better fitted for it than for any other. What do you think of the profession, Miss Morris?"

"I have always thought, that if it had been for me to choose a profession, I should have preferred the legal one to the clerical, that I might have done good to my country in many ways which are only open to the lawyer or the states man," replied Beulah.

And Winthrop Whately's decision was fixed for the law.

After a week delightfully spent at Baxter, Mrs. Whately and her son took leave of the kind and hospitable family at the farm-house, and were on their journey homeward.

Not a word had been spoken for several miles. At length Mrs. Whately remarked, "Winthrop, you are a dull companion this morning."

"Ma'am! What is it? Did you speak to me?" said he, startled from his reverie.

"I merely said that you were very dull this morning."

"I am at your service; what shall we talk about?"

"Beulah Morris," was the direct reply. "What do you think of her?"

"That chimes in very well with my own thoughts, for it was of her I was thinking. She is the most lady-like girl that I ever saw in America."

"And I think you are quite cured of your partiality for foreign manners by remaining so long abroad."

"I like American manners when they are not spoiled by affectation, and an attempt to imitate foreigners. I wish our people would be more independent in that respect. They ought not to despise themselves because, forsooth, every Englishman who darts through the country sees fit to ridicule their manners for differing from his own. Just so they have always ridiculed French, Italian, and Dutch manners. John Bull, after all his pretensions, is not the standard for the world, in this respect."

"I am glad you like the manners of my young friend. They are simple American manners, yet I never saw her do a rude or uncivil thing, nor heard her speak an impolite word while she was with me. Her gracefulness, too, was remarked by every one who saw her; she alone was unconscious of i."

"Why did you not tell me more about Beulah, mother, mine? I thought she was a girl of thirteen or fourteen by the way you spoke of her before we left home."

"I think it injudicious to praise an absent friend too highly; I never do it. I seldom spoke of you while you were absent," said Mrs. Whately.

"I am glad you did not, for when Beulah Morris is a little older, I may want to speak to her for myself in a cause that will involve deeper interest to me than any with which my future clients will ever intrust me."

"You have my best wishes for your success, Winthrop," said his mother. "Many have I seen as polished and refined as that lovely girl, some more beautiful, and others more intellectual, but never one who acted out so clearly the all-pervading principle of her life, 'Do unto others as you would that others should do unto you.' 'Whatsoever things in her are pure, lovely, or of good report,' flow from this divine principle, and render her the true Christian lady."

THE END.

www.ingramcontent.com/pod-product-compliance
Lightning Source LLC
LaVergne TN
LVHW050533100826
845148LV00002B/547

9781425519117